The Big Platter Cookbook

Cooking and Entertaining Family Style

Lou Jane Temple and **A. Cort Sinnes**

Photographs by Steven Rothfeld

Stewart, Tabori & Chang
New York

For our daughters, Reagan and Brooke
May the Big Platter spirit live on

Published by
STEWART, TABORI & CHANG
115 West 18th Street
New York, NY 10011

Canadian Distribution:
Canadian Manda Group
One Atlantic Avenue, Suite 105
Toronto, Ontario M6K 3E7
CANADA

10 9 8 7 6 5 4 3 2 1

First Printing

Stewart, Tabori & Chang is a subsidiary of

LA MARTINIÈRE GROUPE

Library of Congress Cataloging-in-Publication Data
Temple, Lou Jane.
The big platter cookbook : cooking and entertaining family style / Lou Jane Temple and A. Cort Sinnes ; photographs by Steven Rothfeld.
    p. cm.
    Includes index.
    ISBN 1-58479-332-5
1. Quantity cookery. 2. Entertaining. I. Sinnes, A. Cort. II. Title.
TX820.T412 2004
641.5'7—dc22   2004048236

Design by Pamela Geismar
Food styling by David Shalleck

Printed in Singapore

Contents

Introduction

From the moment the door opened, it was apparent that something was very wrong.

It was Memorial Day weekend and a group of us—all old friends—had been invited to another friend's house for what we thought was dinner. Five of us had carpooled, so we all arrived at the front door together. When the host opened the door, he rolled his eyes heavenward, and said "It's about time. Come on in." The hostess was in the kitchen, obviously peeved. The five of us looked nervously at each other, poured drinks, and quickly discovered that owing to a classic miscommunication, we were approximately three hours late (The term "early dinner" was the culprit—what meant two o'clock to them meant five o'clock to us). Ouch.

By the time the second round of drinks was in progress, apologies had been proffered and the group had regained its collective conviviality and good humor. What followed can only be described as a revelation: The fact that we were several hours late meant that our hosts had plenty of time (and then some) to get the meal completely ready to serve, from appetizers through dessert. Foil was taken off a couple of platters of starters and placed on a big outdoor table; the rest of the food was served with ease on more big platters. Because there was nothing to do in the kitchen, the host and hostess actually sat with us, relaxed and talkative. I noticed how pleasant it was that no one had to jump up and down from the table, running to and from the kitchen and generally making themselves absent from the party.

Although the get-together was uncomfortable at first, we all learned a valuable lesson: If you prepare the kinds of foods that can be made ahead of time and present them in a casual, help-yourself style, it's possible for the hosts to have as much fun as the guests. Once the ice was broken, our hosts remarked how relaxing and enjoyable the party was for them. From that day on, I resolved to try to create the same sort of comfort and ease as a host and cook in my own home. The concept of Big Platter cooking and entertaining was born.

Most of the recipes offered on the following pages are as good hot as they are served at room temperature, or cool. Lidia Bastianich, owner of Felidia in New York City and Lidia's in Kansas City, once told me she preferred food meant to be served at room temperature: "If it's too hot or too cold, you can't taste all the flavors," she said. It was a point well taken, one which we kept in mind as we developed the recipes in this book. From grilled meats and seafood, to hearty ethnic specialties and vegetarian entrees, the majority of our Big Platter fare can be prepared ahead, arranged on generous platters or even more generous bowls, and enjoyed when you and your guests are ready to eat.

Last, but hardly least, the very nature of Big Platter cooking and entertaining embodies a generosity of spirit and the spirit of generosity. It is distinctly unfussy, full-flavored, and homey. To family and friends, it says "Come in, sit down, make yourself at home—there's plenty of room and plenty to eat. Enjoy!"

Here's to homemade fun, full platters, and tables filled with the sounds of contented friendship.

A.C.S.
Calistoga, California, 2004

I believe the pleasures of the table are somewhat mystical. Sharing a meal has sacred properties in my book, elevating a common need for fuel into a common sharing of life. After all, what else does every human being agree upon except that they would like to eat every day—and heartily—if possible? Sharing a meal is the best way for us to recognize each other's humanness. When we look across the table at our fellow diners while enjoying the same comforting food and drink, we can easily appreciate our sameness.

Of course, mystical and sacred don't describe most of our everyday meals. Our four-year-olds will only eat white food, our teenagers nuke frozen pizzas, and we eat peanut butter on toast in front of the computer (my personal favorite).

That's exactly why we wanted to write this book. Sometimes a meal is just a fueling-up pit stop. In order to multi-task, we nibble on cheese and crackers at our desk, microwave ramon noodles, or drive through the fast food line: we need to get where we need to go and be recharged at the same time. I do all of the above, just like you.

But I know what it feels like when you make a nice dinner and everyone is sitting down together, enjoying conversation, plenty of food, and maybe some good wine. Those moments, whether with friends or family or your romantic partner, those moments are the best.

Think back over the important events in your life and most likely you'll realize that a meal was an essential component. Your wedding, your Bar Mitzvah, the funeral of a beloved grandparent, the baptism of your child. Sharing a meal seals the deal. We hope that the recipes in this book will help you to "seal the deal" again and again.

Learning to cook saved me. Suddenly, barely old enough to wear lipstick, I became a pregnant teenage bride. I had never done one thing around the house, never even made my own bed or washed a dish. My father had a dime store with a wonderful lunch counter so I hadn't bothered to learn about cooking. But when I found myself adrift in a world I didn't understand, I started to teach myself to cook. I made pancakes from the recipe on the box of Bisquick and was so happy when they were edible, not realizing the concoction was essentially foolproof. I tackled lemon meringue pie that first year and pizza out of the Chef Boy Ardee box (with sausage added), and started producing a respectable pot roast. When my college student husband became a teacher, I invited every teacher in the school district over for a Christmas party—cookies and nonalcoholic eggnog, as I recall.

I had discovered that when I cooked, I didn't feel so out of place. It connected me with other humans. It still does.

L.J.T.
Kansas City, Missouri, 2004
ljtpink@sbcglobal.net

How to Use This Book

It is wonderful to prepare a good meal and share it with people you care about. But we know that making the time, making the food, making it all happen can feel daunting. That's where Big Platter cooking and entertaining comes in. We've organized the one-hundred-plus recipes in this book into seasonal chapters, and added separate chapters on starters and desserts. Unless otherwise noted, each recipe serves eight to twelve, so you can mix and match as you choose.

If you want menu suggestions, we've sprinkled inspiration throughout the book including ideas for a Do-Ahead Cocktail Party, an All-American Barbecue, and even a Mardi Gras Party. But there is ample opportunity for you to construct your own menus, as simple or elaborate as you choose. Each of the entrees is paired with a wine tip to help you round out any meal in style. A section on Big Platter Pots, Pans, and Platters closes the book; there you'll find suggestions for cookware and platters that will help you make and serve these dishes with ease.

Master two or three of the good-tasting, flavorful recipes in each season and you'll want to cook them for your loved ones.

Sharing a meal and the moment is what it's all about. We hope this book makes that a little easier.

Big Platter Starters

We aren't much on fancy starters. It goes against the Big Platter philosophy to serve tiny, fussy hors d'oeuvres that take lots of prep time and must be passed on trays. And starters that must be heated or fried are going to need your attention just when you should be paying attention to your guests. It is nice, however, to have something out for those guests who arrive starved. And if you are serving alcohol, it is always good to begin serving food at the same time. So, here are some easy Big Platter starters. Most of these can be prepared ahead of time; put them on a platter just as your guests arrive and you're done.

Satay with Tamarind Dipping Sauce

Satay has become a common starter in restaurants, and it's a great home party dish too. Even though it requires grilling, and thus some attention, satay doesn't have to be hot off the grill to be good. Make it an hour or so before your guests arrive and it will be even more flavorful at serving time. Choose between chicken, pork, or beef, or serve all three.

CHICKEN

6 to 8 boneless, skinless chicken breast halves (3 to 4 pounds total)

1 can (13.5 ounces) coconut milk

1/2 cup Thai sweet chili sauce

2 tablespoons toasted sesame oil

PORK

2 pork tenderloins (2 1/2 pounds total)

1/2 cup sriracha sauce (a chili-garlic sauce; the most common brand has a rooster on the label)

1 cup dry to semidry sherry

Juice of 2 limes

BEEF

1 flank steak (1 1/2 to 2 pounds)

1/2 cup soy sauce

1/4 cup sriracha chili-garlic sauce

2 tablespoons creamy peanut butter

1 tablespoon vegetable oil

1 recipe Tamarind Dipping Sauce (recipe follows)

To prepare the chicken

1. Rinse the chicken breast halves and pat them dry with paper towels. Cut them lengthwise into 3/8-inch-thick strips.

2. Place these strips in a single layer on a piece of wax paper or plastic wrap. Cover with another piece of paper or film and pound the strips flat with the flat side of a cleaver or meat pounder.

3. Combine the coconut milk, chili sauce, and sesame oil in a large Ziploc bag or storage container. Add the chicken strips and let them marinate in the refrigerator for 2 hours or overnight.

4. Bring to room temperature before grilling. String the strips on bamboo skewers, weaving the meat accordion style.

To prepare the pork

Cut thin strips of the pork tenderloin, about 3/8 inch thick, at an angle. Depending on the size of the tenderloin, you should have 15 to 25 slices. Combine the sriracha sauce, sherry, and lime juice and then the pork in a large Ziploc bag or storage container. Marinate in the refrigerator for at least 2 hours but not more than 3 hours or the citrus juice will start "cooking" the pork. Finish as with the chicken.

To prepare the beef

Cut thin strips of the steak, about 3/8 inch thick, against the grain. Combine the soy sauce, sriracha sauce, peanut butter and oil and then the steak in a large Ziploc bag or storage container and marinate in the refrigerator for 2 hours or overnight. Bring to room temperature and finish as with the chicken.

To grill

1. Prepare a hot grill, either charcoal or gas-fired.

2. Grill satays directly over the hot fire. The pork will take slightly longer than the chicken or beef. Count on 4 to 6 minutes per side for the chicken and beef, depending on the desired state of doneness. Add a minute or two per side for the pork. Serve hot off the grill with Tamarind Dipping Sauce.

Tamarind Dipping Sauce

1. Combine ingredients in a heavy saucepan, and bring to a boil.

2. Reduce heat and simmer for 20 to 30 minutes, until the sauce has reduced and thickened to a light, syrupy consistency.

3. To remove the ginger and lemon grass, pour the sauce through a strainer into a serving dish. Serve hot or at room temperature.

1 can (12 ounces) tamarind nectar

2-inch piece of fresh ginger, peeled and diced

6-inch piece of lemon grass, smashed with the flat side of a chef's knife or cleaver

2 tablespoons rice wine vinegar

2 tablespoons brown sugar

1 tablespoon sesame oil

Smoked Trout Mousse

Smoked trout is the cleanest-tasting smoked fish, probably because of the low fat content. It also seems the most elegant, especially when suspended in cream cheese and heavy cream. If you want, you can make a slimmer version using low-fat ricotta in place of the cream cheese, but you do need to use real cream. Keep this on hand during the winter holidays, just in case someone drops by with a bottle of chilled champagne.

Puree all ingredients in a food processor. Put in a mold or ramekin and chill at least 2 hours. Serve with crackers or little toasts. Refrigerated, this mousse will last a week.

2 smoked trout fillets (about 1 pound total)

1 pound cream cheese

1 tablespoon dried dill

¼ cup heavy cream

Juice of 1 lemon

Dash of paprika

Grilled Oysters

Oysters are the easiest of the bivalves to cook directly over a fire. Although large oysters may be shucked, drained, and cooked on skewers (they will shrink considerably, an advantage if the oysters are especially big), it's far easier to simply cook unopened oysters in the shells. As if by magic, they will open by themselves. Make sure to place them on the grill flat shell up so the bottom cupped shell can hold the oyster's liquor and the garlicky butter sauce.

---

1. Scrub the oysters well and store them, flat shell up, in the shallow pan until ready to cook. Cover with the damp towel; do not store in water.

2. Prepare a hot fire in a charcoal or gas grill.

3. Combine the butter, garlic, lemon juice, and hot sauce in a saucepan. Simmer over low heat while the oysters are on the grill.

4. Place the oysters directly over the hot fire, flat shell up, and cover the grill. Have a pair of oven mitts and an oyster knife at the ready. As soon as the oyster shells pop open, about 3 minutes, remove them from the fire, and open them completely with the oyster knife, discarding the top shell and any oysters that did not open. Add a spoonful of the butter sauce to the cup of each oyster and put them back on the grill until the liquid is bubbly and the oysters begin to shrink and curl at the edges, 2 to 3 minutes.

5. Serve immediately. In all truthfulness, the oysters probably won't even make it to a big platter: true oyster lovers are content to hover around the grill, popping them in their mouths as soon as they are ready!

4 dozen large oysters in their shells

2 cups (4 sticks) butter, melted

8 large garlic cloves, pushed through a garlic press

Juice of 2 lemons

Tabasco or other hot sauce to taste

Shallow pan or bucket

Damp towel or burlap

Oyster knife

Low-Fat Squash Dip

This squash dip may be low in fat, but it's so full flavored you won't feel deprived. If you want, trade the fat grams you save for crispy corn chips or toasted pita wedges. Whatever you use, it needs to be crispy to contrast with the silky texture of the dip.

3 acorn squash, or 1 medium to large butternut squash

Nonstick baking spray

1 jar (16 ounces) salsa (almost every brand is low- or nonfat, but check the label to make sure)

1/4 cup fresh cilantro leaves, chopped

1. Preheat the oven to 400°F. Split the squash in half and discard the seeds.

2. Bake the squash, split side down, on a baking sheet that has been sprayed with nonstick cooking spray, until the squash is very soft when pricked with a fork, about 30 minutes. Let it cool and remove the skin.

3. Combine the salsa, cilantro, and cooked squash in a food processor or large bowl. Puree with the food processor or with a fork for a chunky texture. This dip will keep 3 to 5 days if refrigerated.

Note: Try making baked chips instead of buying fried ones. Cut thin corn or flour tortillas into wedges, drizzle with a little oil and kosher salt, and bake at 325°F until the chips are crisp, about 10 minutes.

Feta Spread

Delicious on crackers, this spread also makes a great vegetarian sandwich filling. Spread it on some good bread and top with tomato, cucumbers, sprouts, and lettuce or arugula.

1 pound feta cheese, crumbled (Bulgarian feta, if it's available)

4 hard-boiled eggs, grated on the coarse side of a grater

3 to 4 cloves garlic, peeled and minced

1/2 teaspoon each of freshly cracked pepper and dried dill

6 ounces (about 3/4 cup) sour cream

1. Place all ingredients in a large bowl and mix well. Tear off about a 2-foot piece of plastic wrap. Mound the feta mixture in the center of the plastic wrap and pull up the edges to cover tightly. Refrigerate for at least 2 hours (overnight is preferable).

2. When ready to serve, transfer the cheese mixture to a plate, smoothing it with a rubber spatula if necessary, and serve with toasted pita wedges, water crackers, or baked bagel slices.

You don't have to imbibe to notice that cocktail parties are back with an energy that's all their own. There's no need to fix a full-fledged dinner for your guests, and most parties last only two hours. With these make-ahead recipes, you'll be ready when the doors open. Limit the cocktail to one well-chosen item, then offer white wine, beer, and soft drinks.

§ **Chutney Cream Cheese Spread**
§ **Home-Smoked Salmon**
§ **Artichoke Hummus**
§ **Country Pâté with Prunes and Hazelnuts**
§ **Bruschetta Platter**
§ **Crudités with Spicy Peanut Dip**

Wine Tip: In addition to your cocktail of the day, whether it's daiquiris or martinis, offer a Sauvignon Blanc. It will taste so much better with the nibbles than a Chardonnay.

Chutney Cream Cheese Spread

Obviously, this recipe will serve many more than eight to twelve people, but this ratio of flavorings to cream cheese seems to be the best. You might try it with a pound of cream cheese and see how you like it. You'll find that even this large, economy version disappears fast from the refrigerator. It lasts about five days—we've even eaten it happily after a week—but the green onion becomes stronger as time goes on. Serve in the middle of a round platter with water crackers, wheat crackers, or a combination. This spread makes a delicious sandwich filling combined with slices of turkey or ham.

1. Combine all the ingredients in a mixing bowl, making sure to cut up any large pieces of mango in the chutney.

2. Shape into two small mounds or a single large one. Wrap in plastic wrap and refrigerate. Chill at least 2 hours or overnight.

$1\frac{1}{2}$ **pounds cream cheese, at room temperature**

1 jar (12 ounces) Major Grey's chutney, or any other good mango chutney

1 bunch green onions, all of the white and part of the green, thinly sliced

$\frac{1}{2}$ **cup each of golden raisins and chopped roasted peanuts (salted or not)**

1 small can (8 ounces) crushed pineapple, drained

1 tablespoon mild curry powder

Home-Smoked Salmon

One of the preparations we wanted to perfect for this book was home-smoked salmon—not-too-dry, not-too-moist, flavorful, just-smoky-enough salmon. And just as important was a recipe using a covered kettle grill instead of a commercial smoker. After more than 20 years of experimentation, we think we can say we've achieved that goal. Our home-smoked salmon can be used either as a traditional hors d'oeuvre or, somewhat surprisingly, as an entree. However, you'll probably eat enough of it as an hors d'oeuvre you won't want an entree!

1 cup kosher salt

1 cup sugar

2 cups hot water

5 cups cold water

1 side (fillet) of salmon (2½ to 3 pounds), skin on

Mild vegetable oil, such as canola

Very finely ground white pepper to taste

Paprika to taste

1-gallon Ziploc bag

Heavy-duty aluminum foil

Charcoal briquettes

Smoking chips (see Note)

1. Fill the Ziploc bag with the salt, sugar, and hot water. Zip the bag and massage the brine mixture until the salt and sugar are dissolved. Add the cold water to the bag. Put the salmon in the brine, zip the bag shut, and place it in the refrigerator for 3 to 4 hours.

2. Toward the end of the brining period, ignite approximately 36 charcoal briquettes on one side of a covered kettle grill.

3. Remove the salmon from the brine; blot it dry with several layers of paper towels. Place the salmon on a double layer of aluminum foil and rub both sides with a few tablespoons of oil. Dust the flesh side with white pepper and paprika.

4. Place approximately 2 cups of the smoking chips in a double layer of heavy-duty aluminum foil, fold into a tight packet, and poke a few holes into the top with the tip of a knife.

5. Once the briquettes are covered with a light gray ash, place the packet of smoking chips directly on top of the briquettes. Put the cooking grate in the grill and slide the salmon off the foil onto the grate on the side opposite the briquettes. (To make it easier to remove the salmon once it is done, place the salmon lengthwise, perpendicular to the grill rods.) Cover the grill, leaving both the top and bottom vents completely open. Position the lid so the vents are over the salmon, which helps to pull the smoke through the fish. Allow the salmon to cook for approximately 2 hours, or until the fire goes out. Avoid taking the lid off during the cooking period.

6. Using two spatulas, remove the salmon from the grill. If it sticks here and there, turn a spatula upside down and wedge it under the salmon, gently nudging the entire salmon free of the grate. Once the salmon is off the grate, turn it over, skin side up, and remove the skin; it will come off easily if you lift it with the tip of a sharp knife from either the head or tail end.

7. Serve home-smoked salmon warm off the grill, or chilled. It is absolutely delicious as is, or for hors d'oeuvres, accompanied with melba toast (or any other flat bread or cracker), finely chopped white onion, capers, and lemon wedges. If you serve the salmon as an entree, simple wedges of lemon will suffice.

Note: Alder wood is the favored smoke note to add to salmon, a tradition begun eons ago by Native American Indians from the Pacific Northwest. Apple wood is a close second (if you use apple wood from your own trees, make sure no chemical pesticides or fungicides have been used on them). If you can't find either alder wood or apple smoking chips, the more widely available oak or hickory will do nicely.

Artichoke Hummus

This version of hummus came about when we thought there was a jar of tahini (sesame paste) in the pantry and there wasn't. With no time to shop, we substituted a can of artichoke hearts instead and have never looked back. The fat content goes way down and the flavor is terrific.

1. Combine all ingredients but the oil in the bowl of a food processor and turn it on.

2. Slowly drizzle the olive oil into the bowl as the ingredients are being processed to a creamy consistency. Serve with pita wedges.

1 can (15 ounces) garbanzo beans, drained

1 can (13 ounces) artichoke hearts, drained and cut in half

3 to 6 cloves peeled garlic, to your taste

Juice of 2 lemons

1/2 teaspoon each of paprika, ground cumin, and kosher salt

Ground white pepper to taste

Olive oil, enough to achieve desired consistency

Country Pâté with Prunes and Hazelnuts

Everyone should have a pâté in their cooking repertoire. This mild version is inspired by a Julia Child recipe, but we replaced the liver with ground veal and the onions with shallots, then added the layers of prunes and hazelnuts. Serve with crackers or toasts made from skinny baguettes. To improve the pâté's density and texture, you allow it to cool, cover it with plastic wrap, and weight it with a brick or large can while it chills. Because of this final step, this pâté is best made the day before you intend to serve it.

3 tablespoons butter

4 shallots, peeled, sliced, and minced

2 cloves garlic, peeled and minced

1 pound each of ground chicken breast meat, ground veal, and ground pork (grind them in a food processor or ask your butcher to do it)

2 eggs, beaten

5 ounces goat cheese

1 cup fresh breadcrumbs, packed

3 tablespoons brandy

1 tablespoon kosher salt

1/2 teaspoon each of ground allspice, ground cardamom, and freshly ground pepper

1/4 teaspoon dried thyme, or 1 tablespoon fresh thyme leaves

About 18 dried, pitted prunes

1/2 cup hazelnuts, lightly toasted (see Note)

Nonstick baking spray, for the pan

1. Preheat the oven to 350°F. Melt the butter in a small sauté pan and sauté the shallots and garlic until soft, 7 to 10 minutes.

2. Combine the sautéed shallots and garlic and everything but the prunes and hazelnuts in a large mixing bowl.

3. Put one-third of this meat mixture in a loaf pan that has been sprayed with nonstick baking spray. Smooth the top of the mixture with a spatula. Cover with the lightly toasted hazelnuts. Add another third of the meat mixture, again patting the surface smooth. Place the pitted prunes on top of this layer, about three to a row, six rows total. Cover with the remaining meat mixture.

4. Place the pâté-filled pan in a larger pan. Fill the larger pan with water until the liquid is about halfway up the side of the smaller pan. Bake for 1 1/2 hours, or until the juices are almost clear.

5. Cool the pâté for an hour, cover it with plastic wrap, then weight it with a brick or a large, heavy can. Refrigerate overnight.

6. Remove the pâté from the refrigerator and discard the plastic wrap. Run a sharp knife around the perimeter of the pâté. Cover the pan with a serving platter and flip the pan and the platter upside down. The pâté will slip out of the pan, ready for slicing.

Note: To toast the hazelnuts, spread them on a baking sheet with a lip and toast them in a preheated 350°F oven for 10 to 12 minutes, until the meat of the nuts is slightly browned. Put the nuts in a clean tea towel and rub them. About 75 percent of the brown, paper-thin inner skins will come off on the towel and that is usually enough.

Bruschetta Platter

This rustic dish is easy and satisfying to make on a grill, either charcoal or gas-fired. We've yet to run across anyone who didn't love it. The nice thing about using Roma (paste) tomatoes is that no matter what time of year, there always seem to be good-quality ones available. This recipe serves eight, but adjust the yield depending on the size of your crowd.

1. Rinse the tomatoes, place them in a row, and spear them with two parallel bamboo skewers. (This will keep them from spinning around when you turn them on the grill.)

2. Prepare a medium-hot grill, either charcoal or gas-fired. Grill the skewered tomatoes directly over the fire, 5 minutes per side.

3. Remove the tomatoes from the grill once they begin to soften. Peel the skins (they will pull off easily) and roughly chop the tomatoes. Place them in a serving bowl. Add the garlic, chopped basil, olive oil, and capers, and season with salt and pepper. Toss lightly.

4. Split the bread in half lengthwise then halve again widthwise to create more manageable pieces. Add the anchovy paste, if using, to the melted butter and mix well. Brush the cut sides of the bread with the butter or butter and anchovy mixture. Place the bread, cut sides down, over the medium-hot grill. Toast both sides of the bread; this will only take a couple of minutes so watch it carefully.

5. Cut the grilled bread into 1-inch-wide strips and place them on a platter alongside the bowl of seasoned grilled tomatoes. Heap the tomatoes onto the slices of grilled bread and enjoy.

9 large Roma tomatoes (about 3 pounds)

2 to 3 cloves garlic, peeled and minced

¼ cup chopped fresh basil leaves

1 tablespoon extra-virgin olive oil

2 tablespoons capers, rinsed and drained

Kosher salt and freshly ground pepper to taste

1 loaf crusty Italian or French bread

1 tablespoon anchovy paste, if desired

3 tablespoons melted butter

Crudités with Spicy Peanut Dip

We weren't going to include yet another recipe for peanut dip until we saw a group of folks standing around a platter of jicama, red pepper strips, and blanched green beans with a bowl of peanut dip in the middle. They weren't moving, just shoveling it in and smiling. That's when we realized you all should have this recipe. The key ingredient is Thai sweet chili sauce (the bottle sometimes reads "Thai sweet chili sauce for chicken"), a prepared product available in Asian markets around the country. (We even checked in Salina, Kansas, and there it was on the shelf.) The choice of crudités is up to you. We like the three vegetables mentioned above, or when asparagus is good in the spring, just blanched asparagus.

---

1 large bottle (25 ounces) Thai sweet chili sauce

4 cups roasted peanuts, salted or not

¼ cup toasted sesame oil

¼ to ½ cup hot water

1. Put the chili sauce in the bowl of your food processor and turn it on.

2. Slowly pour the peanuts into the food processor until you reach the stage of stiff peanut butter. This should take about 4 cups, give or take a few peanuts.

3. While the machine is still going, slowly add the oil and the water until you reach a good dipping consistency. You will want to stop the machine and scrape down the sides of the bowl at least once during processing. The whole thing takes about 5 minutes.

4. Store the dip in a covered container in the refrigerator and serve with your choice of raw or blanched vegetables. Bring to room temperature before serving for the fullest flavor. Keeps for 2 to 3 weeks.

Big Platter Fall

In most regions of the country, fall marks the end of the growing season. So in the kitchen our focus changes too. The menus are heartier, deeper somehow. The leafy green vegetables of summer are replaced with root vegetables on our tables. The fruits we enjoyed so abundantly just weeks ago are now savored in dried and preserved forms. We long for the aroma of a rich meat dish wafting through the house from the kitchen. We are settling in. It's a perfect time to cook a pot of Beef Zinfandel and invite our friends over to share it.

Beef Zinfandel

In this California version of the classic French boeuf bourguignon, we replaced the French Burgundy with Zinfandel, a variety of grape native to California—or at least a variety that came to California from somewhere else and flourished in its new home. Dredging the stew meat with flour before browning helps to thicken the sauce as it cooks and adds little crispy bits that sure are good. Serve this stew with steamed new potatoes, rice, or egg noodles.

2 yellow onions, peeled

1 bottle (about 750 ml) red Zinfandel

3 to 4 cloves garlic, peeled and smashed with a large knife

2 teaspoons whole black peppercorns, smashed

3 to 4 whole cloves

Kosher salt to taste

2 tablespoons olive oil

4 pounds beef stew meat

¼ cup vegetable oil

1 cup flour seasoned with 1 teaspoon each of salt, pepper, and paprika

4 to 6 strips bacon, diced

2 stalks celery, finely minced

1 large carrot, finely minced

1 can (14 ounces) chicken or beef broth

½ teaspoon dried thyme

¼ teaspoon dried rosemary

1 pound white button mushrooms, sliced

2 cups small white onions, fresh or frozen

1. Slice one of the onions and place it in a large bowl. Pour in one-half of the bottle of wine and add the garlic, peppercorns, cloves, salt, and olive oil. Add the beef stew meat and mix to coat all the pieces. Marinate at room temperature for at least 2 hours, or overnight in the refrigerator.

2. To make the stew, heat the vegetable oil in a large, heavy sauce-pan over medium heat. Put the seasoned flour in a large flat bowl. Dredge individual pieces of the marinated meat in the flour, and then brown them on all sides, about 6 minutes. Set the browned meat and the remaining marinade aside.

3. To the same pan, add the diced bacon and brown it. Set the bacon aside, removing it from the pan with tongs or a slotted spoon. Mince the remaining onion and add it, along with the celery and carrot, to the bacon grease. Sauté over low heat until just soft, about 8 minutes.

4. In a Dutch oven or large roasting pan, combine the browned meat and the sautéed vegetables, along with the remaining half bottle of Zinfandel, the reserved marinade, beef broth, thyme, and rosemary. Cover the pan and keep it just at a simmer for 2 hours. If you are doing this in the oven, bake in a preheated 350°F for 2 hours.

5. After 2 hours, add the mushrooms and small white onions. Simmer, uncovered, for an additional hour.

Wine Tip: Serve with the same Zinfandel you cooked with.

Escarole, Potato, and Sausage à la **Tamborello**

Lulu is a member of a group called the Barbecue Queens. They are mostly food professionals in Kansas City who occasionally do contest-cooking—that's competition barbecuing—usually to benefit a charity. When we told them about the *Big Platter Cookbook,* one of Lulu's fellow Queens, Jean Tamburello, gave us this recipe. She said it was a great Big Platter dish, good and easy. She was right.

---

1. Heat the olive oil in a Dutch oven or large, heavy pot over medium-low heat. Sauté the onions and garlic; when the onions start to wilt, add the sausages. Let the sausage pieces brown, 10 to 15 minutes.

2. Add the potatoes and peppers and enough water or stock, about 3 or 4 cups, to almost cover the sausages, potatoes, and peppers. Put the chopped escarole on top and season with salt, pepper, and the red pepper flakes. Cover and simmer for 20 minutes, stirring occasionally. Uncover and cook an additional 20 minutes.

3. Mound the stew in a large platter with a lip and drizzle with olive oil and a splash of vinegar. We used sherry vinegar, but red wine vinegar or balsamic would be good, as well.

Wine Tip: Salice Salentino. If you haven't discovered this inexpensive red wine from the Adriatic side of Italy, this is the time. It is a wonderful food wine. The late, great Cosimo Taurino—whose winery produces one of the best Salice Salentinos—is Lulu's favorite producer.

2 tablespoons olive oil

2 onions, peeled and sliced

4 to 6 cloves garlic, peeled and sliced

3 pounds Italian sausage, hot, sweet, or a combination, cut into 2-inch pieces

2 pounds small new potatoes, rinsed

3 colored bell peppers (red, yellow, and orange if possible), seeded and cut into wedges

3 to 4 cups water, or vegetable or chicken stock

3 heads escarole, rinsed and coarsely chopped

Kosher salt and freshly ground pepper to taste

1 teaspoon crushed red pepper flakes

Extra-virgin olive oil and sherry vinegar, for drizzling

Cort's Thanksgiving

There are few holidays when each family adheres more closely to its own traditions than Thanksgiving. Whatever dishes you grew up with—whether they include cornbread stuffing, creamed onions, or string bean casserole made with onion soup mix—it's difficult to change any aspect without howls of complaint. If, however, you're brave enough to try something different, the following menu is so good it just might become a "new" family tradition.

§ **Pandora's Turkey**
§ **Fresh Cranberry and Tangerine Relish**
§ **Succotash**
§ **Roasted Beets and Carrots with Orange-Ginger Sauce**
§ **Lulu's Root Bake**
§ **Aunt Mayme's Date Pudding (page 182)**

Wine Tip: Oregon Pinot Noir and German Riesling both have the balance and acidity that's well-suited to turkey.

Pandora's Turkey

Do you want to serve the best turkey you've ever eaten this Thanksgiving? Do you want to sleep in Thanksgiving morning, instead of getting up at 6 A.M. to put the turkey in the oven? All you need to accomplish this seemingly magical feat is a covered kettle grill, a 5-pound bag of charcoal, and the turkey. Note: If Thanksgiving Day dawns really cold and blustery, roll the grill to some protected spot close to the house, like the back porch.

In our households, charcoal roasting (this is technically what you are doing—not grilling or barbecuing) is the preferred method for cooking any turkey, no matter what time of year it is. We've cooked at least a hundred turkeys this way—so many that we finally gave the procedure a name, Pandora's Turkey, which refers to the fact that you don't, under any circumstances, take the lid off the grill until the fire goes out. Pandora's Turkey turns out beautifully brown and crisp on the outside, moist on the inside (just the way you've always wanted it), and makes the entire neighborhood smell heavenly in the process. The extraordinary part of this procedure is that since we discovered it, we've never had a turkey take more than three hours to cook completely.

A serious warning: cooking an 18- to 22-pound turkey in three hours or less makes most people nervous, including your guests. So don't tell Aunt Hattie that the turkey took so little time to cook until after she's taken her first bite and pronounced it the moistest, most delicious turkey she's ever tasted. Otherwise, she may insist that you put the turkey in the oven, not that contraption in the backyard, and cook it until it's really done.

1. Before you begin, read the charcoal-roasting tips on page 26. Start with a clean grill, free of old coals and ash. Ignite 5 pounds of briquettes. Five pounds may seem like a lot, but this is a special procedure. If you have difficulty determining 5 pounds, simply buy a 10-pound bag of charcoal and use half.

2. While you're waiting for the coals to catch, prepare the turkey for stuffing. Remove the neck and giblets from inside the bird; reserve them for making the gravy, if desired. Wash the bird thoroughly with cold water. Pat dry with a paper towel, both inside and out. Place the turkey in the aluminum roasting pan.

3. Put the onions and celery in a large bowl and mix with the poultry seasoning. Place a handful of this aromatic mixture inside the neck cavity. Pull the skin over the cavity and fasten it closed using a small metal or bamboo skewer. Put the rest of the mixture in the body cavity and fasten closed with another skewer. Secure the legs to the tail using the metal fastener found on most store-bought turkeys.

4. Rub the entire surface of the turkey with vegetable oil. Sprinkle liberally with salt and pepper.

5. Check the fire. The coals are just right when they are completely covered with fine, gray ash. Once at that stage (usually in 20 to 25 minutes), push them to both sides of the fire grate in equal quantities, leaving the center free of briquettes. Put the cooking grill in place. Position the roasting pan and turkey in the middle of the grill and put the grill lid on. Leave both the top and bottom vents completely open.

6. Within minutes you will start to hear some action in the roasting pan and smell that delightful aroma. The turkey will be done when the coals have burned out, usually around 2½ to 3 hours.

7. Remove the lid—finally—and voilà! A beautifully roasted, mahogany brown, crisp-on-the outside, moist-on-the-inside turkey. Carefully move the bird from the roasting pan to the carving board, and remove and discard the aromatic stuffing, or reserve it for making turkey stock. Let the turkey rest for 20 to 30 minutes, loosely tented with foil. This allows the juices to return to the interior of the meat and makes the turkey much easier to carve. Add any juices that accumulate on the carving board to your gravy, or use for moistening the stuffing. After dinner, you'll have one more thing to be thankful for: your oven won't need cleaning!

---

1 large turkey (18 to 22 pounds, or larger, if it will fit on your grill, covered)

2 yellow onions, peeled and coarsely chopped

5 stalks celery, coarsely chopped

2 tablespoons poultry seasoning or dried sage

½ cup vegetable oil

Kosher salt or seasoned salt and freshly ground pepper to taste

Covered, kettle-type grill

5 pounds premium-brand charcoal briquettes (not natural, lump charcoal)

Disposable aluminum roasting pan, just big enough to fit the turkey

A few metal or bamboo skewers

Tips for Perfect Charcoal-Roasted Turkey

§ Look for a bird that is as squat as possible; a high breastbone will prevent the lid of the grill from closing completely. Over the years, we've found that turkeys in the 18- to 22-pound range fit best. If you want a larger bird, it's a good idea to do a test before you unwrap the bird. Simply place the turkey on the grill (unlit, of course), and make sure the lid closes completely. (For birds larger than 22 pounds, ignite an extra pound of charcoal and add an additional 30 minutes to the cooking time.)

§ We roast turkeys with an aromatic stuffing that is not meant for eating. If you choose to follow this method and plan on making stock from the turkey carcass afterward, hang on to the aromatic stuffing: it will improve the taste of the stock.

§ There will be plenty of juices in the roasting pan. These can be divided between the gravy pot and the oven-cooked stuffing, in case it gets dry. So far there haven't been any complaints about the stuffing, especially when it's generously moistened with stock. In fact, no one has ever detected that it wasn't cooked inside the bird.

§ Turkeys cooked in covered kettle grills don't need basting. In fact, if you take the lid off to baste the bird (or even just to peek), you'll blow the whole process. The rapid influx of air causes the coals to heat up quickly, resulting in an uneven cooking temperature and shortening the life of the coals. At least that's the only convincing explanation we've been able to come up with. At any rate, leave the lid on the grill until the fire goes out. You know what happened to Pandora when she opened the box....

Fresh Cranberry and Tangerine Relish

This recipe results in a refreshing and unusual flavor combination, just right for serving with the charcoal-roasted turkey. Please note that the relish requires a two-day rest in the refrigerator to mellow the pungency of the fresh tangerine rind.

1. Cut the tangerines in half and remove the seeds. Place half the tangerines and half the cranberries in a food processor fitted with a steel blade. Pulse until the mixture is finely chopped but not pureed. Place the chopped mixture in a large storage container with a tight-fitting lid. Repeat with the remaining cranberries and tangerines.

2. Stir in the sugar and salt. Cover and refrigerate for at least 2 days or up to 2 weeks. Serve cold or at room temperature.

3 tangerines, unpeeled

1 package (12 ounces) fresh cranberries

1 cup sugar

¼ teaspoon kosher salt

Succotash

This is a particularly flavorful variation of a Native American dish that traditionally combines lima beans and corn. If someone in your group just can't abide limas, use red kidney or fava beans instead.

1. Cook the frozen limas according to package directions. If using fresh limas, place them in a saucepan with enough salted water to cover them, bring to a boil, reduce the heat to medium, and cook until just tender, 12 to 15 minutes. Drain.

2. In a large skillet, melt the butter over medium heat. Sauté the chopped onion and red pepper until soft, 6 to 10 minutes. Add the limas and corn kernels and mix well.

3. Add the cream, thyme, salt, pepper, and a dash or two of Tabasco and heat the mixture thoroughly. Place the succotash in a serving dish and sprinkle with the parsley, if using.

2 cups fresh or frozen baby lima beans

2 tablespoons butter

1 medium onion, peeled and diced

½ red bell pepper, seeded and diced

2 cups fresh or frozen corn kernels

½ cup heavy cream

½ teaspoon dried thyme

Kosher salt, freshly ground pepper, and Tabasco to taste

2 tablespoons finely chopped fresh parsley (optional)

Roasted Beets and Carrots with Orange-Ginger Sauce

In the days of the Pilgrims, beets and carrots were of the mammoth variety—the best size for winter storage—and were traditionally roasted over or in the coals. Once you've tried them prepared this way, you'll wonder why we ever stopped. Absolutely delicious!

2 to 3 pounds each of the largest beets and carrots you can find

2 tablespoons mayonnaise

¼ cup fresh orange juice

¼ teaspoon kosher salt

2 large pieces of fresh ginger (enough to yield ½ cup grated)

Fresh parsley, finely chopped (optional)

1. Prepare a hot charcoal grill.

2. Discard the green tops of the beets, if any, and either lay the beets directly on the white-hot briquettes or, if you have enough briquettes, bury the beets in the hot coals. Roast for 45 to 60 minutes, depending on their size (hardball-sized beets will become tender in about 45 minutes). If the beets are resting on top of the coals, turn them once or twice to evenly char them on all sides. Once the beets are tender, remove them from the coals and allow them to cool. When they are cool enough to handle, use a sharp knife to remove the charred skins and slice the roasted beets into ⅜-inch-thick slices.

3. Wash and scrub (but don't peel) the carrots.

4. Place them on the cooking grate, directly over the white-hot coals. Large carrots will cook tender in 35 to 45 minutes. Turn them every 10 to 12 minutes until they're nicely browned on all sides.

5. Allow them to cool slightly and slice lengthwise into ⅜-inch-thick slices.

6. To make the sauce, combine the mayonnaise, orange juice, and salt. Grate the ginger on the large side of a box grater (there's no need to peel it first). Using your hands, gather the grated ginger in a ball and tightly squeeze it over the mayonnaise mixture; you'll be amazed at the amount of juice that comes out. Discard the ginger pulp. Stir the sauce.

7. Arrange the warm beets and carrots on a platter, drizzle with the sauce, and garnish with a little chopped parsley, if desired.

Lulu's **Root Bake**

Lulu's mother was the daughter of Kansas farmers. She was not the least bit sentimental about home cooking and embraced all the newfangled shortcuts that modern life offered: frozen food, cake mix, and other miracles of science. Thus it is with heavy hearts that we confess Lulu's first taste memories of a potato gratin came from a box. Since then she has been on a quest for delicious potato casseroles. This version comes with one tip: keep stepping once you begin the assembling, as the raw potatoes will discolor. You can put the raw potato slices in cold water as you slice them, then dry them off to continue with the recipe. You can also make this a do-ahead casserole by boiling the potatoes and turnips the night before; just reduce the baking time accordingly.

---

1. Spray a large roasting pan with nonstick baking spray.

2. Slice the potatoes in half lengthwise. Place them on a cutting board, cut side down, and cut into very thin slices (approximately ⅛ inch thick). Line the bottom of the roasting pan with overlapping slices of potato. Sprinkle the layer of potatoes evenly with about 1½ tablespoons of the flour and season with salt and pepper. Spread half the cheddar cheese evenly over the potatoes.

3. Slice the peeled turnips in half lengthwise. Place them on a cutting board, cut side down, and cut into thin slices (approximately ⅛ inch thick). Arrange the turnips in overlapping rows over the potato layer. Again, sprinkle evenly with flour and season with salt and pepper. Spread the other half of the cheddar cheese over the turnips.

4. Finish assembling the dish with a final overlapping layer of the sliced potatoes. Sprinkle evenly with salt and pepper to taste. Top with the Parmesan.

5. Heat the half-and-half and cream in a saucepan over low heat and pour the mixture over the potatoes and turnips. Bake for 60 to 90 minutes, depending on the size and depth of the baking dish. Start checking the tenderness of the potatoes after 1 hour; the dish is done when the potatoes pierce easily with a fork.

Nonstick baking spray

3 to 4 pounds large, thin-skinned new potatoes, unpeeled

3 tablespoons flour

Kosher salt and freshly ground pepper (preferably white) to taste

8 ounces firm cheese, such as aged cheddar or Gruyère, grated

1½ to 2 pounds turnips, peeled

4 ounces grating cheese of your choice, such as Parmesan, Asiago, or hard pecorino

2 cups half-and-half

1 cup heavy cream

Cafe Lulu's Macaroni and Cheese

At Cafe Lulu in Kansas City, the menu changed six times a year based on different themes. In the spring it was "March and April in Paris" and featured French bistro food. In August and September it was "Tomato Time," and we made everything you love with homegrown tomatoes. But our macaroni and cheese was one of the things that stayed on the menu year-round, no matter what the theme. One of the reasons for its popularity, aside from the soft spot we all have for comfort food, was that it was made to order, not left sitting in a big hotel pan drying out. When you make this at home, you should keep all the ingredients separate until the very last minute, just before you pop it in the oven, so the pasta doesn't have a chance to soak up the sauce. We like to use orange cheddar so it's a more traditional color, but if you have some good white Vermont cheddar around, use it and enjoy. This serves eight as a main dish and more as a side dish.

1. Cook the macaroni according to package directions and drain it. Pour it into a lightly oiled baking dish of sufficient size and depth to hold the macaroni and cheese mixture. Add the oil to the macaroni and toss to keep it from sticking together. Cover the baking dish with plastic wrap and reserve at room temperature until needed.

2. To make the sauce, melt the butter over medium heat in a medium-sized saucepan. Add the flour and continue cooking, whisking the butter and flour mixture until it has thickened and turned a butter-scotch color. Add the stock and whisk until the mixture is smooth. Add the half-and-half, stirring to blend well.

3. Once the sauce mixture is thoroughly heated, add the three grated cheeses, one at a time. Reduce the heat to low and stir with a wooden spoon until smooth. Add the salt, pepper, and paprika and continue stirring until all the cheese has melted. Remove from heat and reserve until needed (see Note, page 32).

4. To make the topping, open one small corner of the bag of potato chips to let the air out. Using a rolling pin, smash the potato chips while they're still in the bag, taking care not to let crushed chips come out of the open corner of the bag.

5. Melt the butter in a medium-sized frying pan over medium heat. Add the crushed potato chips and Parmesan. Toss gently to thoroughly coat the chips with the butter and cheese mixture.

(continued)

1 pound elbow macaroni

1 tablespoon vegetable oil, plus additional for the baking dish

¼ cup (½ stick) butter

¼ cup flour

2 cups each of chicken stock and half-and-half

½ cup grated Gruyère cheese (about 4 ounces)

1¼ cups grated cheddar cheese, medium or sharp (about 9 ounces)

1 cup grated Parmesan cheese (about 8 ounces)

½ teaspoon each of kosher salt and freshly ground white pepper

¼ teaspoon paprika, sweet or hot

FOR THE TOPPING
1 package (10 ounces) potato chips (regular or spicy)

½ cup (1 stick) butter

½ cup grated Parmesan cheese (about 4 ounces)

6. Preheat the oven to 375°F. Pour the cheese sauce over the macaroni mixture, gently jiggling the baking dish to distribute the sauce evenly. Top with a generous layer of the potato chip mixture, pressing it lightly into the macaroni and cheese. Bake until the cheese sauce bubbles and the top is browned, 50 to 60 minutes, depending on the depth and size of your baking dish. Serve immediately.

Note: The cheese sauce can be made the night before; simply allow the sauce to cool and cover it with plastic wrap, with the plastic actually touching the surface of the sauce. Refrigerate. Allow the sauce to come to room temperature before pouring it over macaroni mixture; it will take a few more minutes to cook than if the sauce were hot. Or if you have a big enough microwavable container, you can heat the sauce in the microwave before you combine it with the pasta.

Wine Tip: One of my favorite food wines is Beaujolais, especially the Cru wines from the villages. The forward fruit taste of a Brouilly should be just right with all this gooey richness.

Blu Lu Salad

When Lulu had her café, this was the most popular item on the menu. This is a salad even children and salad haters can love.

½ cup raspberries, fresh or frozen

⅓ cup raspberry vinegar

⅓ cup honey

1 cup olive oil, or a combination of canola and olive oil

2 heads Boston lettuce, washed, drained, and torn into bite-sized pieces

1 cup crumbled blue cheese

1 cup pecan halves, fried in oil (see Note)

1 cup fresh blueberries

1. Place the raspberries, vinegar, and honey in a food processor. Turn it on and slowly add the oil. The dressing will be thick, and you'll have enough to dress several salads. It will keep for 3 to 4 days in the refrigerator.

2. Place the lettuce in a salad bowl, top with the blue cheese, pecans, and blueberries, and drizzle with the raspberry dressing.

Note: To fry the pecans, heat 2 tablespoons olive oil over medium heat. Add the pecans and toss to coat them with the oil. After 3 to 4 minutes, remove them from the heat and transfer them to a bowl—they will continue to cook if left in the pan. We have burned many a pecan this way.

Cabbage Stuffed with Turkey, Mushrooms, and Barley

Most stuffed cabbage recipes have the same elements. But we spotted one with a mushroom stuffing that led us to add barley...and how about some ground turkey? The next thing we knew, we had a new, rather exotic version of stuffed cabbage. Cort calls this "Stuffed Cabbage Lite." You could easily leave out the turkey for a vegetarian version. And when you make the barley for the filling, you can make extra to serve with the stuffed cabbage.

1. In a big pot of boiling water, parboil the whole head of cabbage. When the outer leaves soften, about 3 minutes, remove the cabbage with tongs, carefully peel off the leaves, keeping each one intact, and put them on a paper towel to dry. Return the cabbage to the boiling water and let the next layer of leaves soften. Continue until the whole head of cabbage has been deconstructed.

2. To make the filling, heat 1 tablespoon each of the butter and oil in a large sauté pan over medium heat and sauté the mushrooms. When the mushrooms are soft, 6 to 7 minutes, remove them from the heat, cool, and mince, remembering they have to be small enough to fit in the cabbage roll.

3. In the same sauté pan, heat the remaining butter and oil and sauté the onion. Add the ground turkey and the bell pepper and cook until the turkey is done, about 10 minutes, remove from the heat.

4. In a large mixing bowl, combine the sautéed mushrooms, turkey mixture, barley, feta cheese, seasonings, and eggs.

5. To make the sauce, heat the butter and oil in a large, heavy saucepan over medium heat. Sauté the mirepoix (onion, carrot, and celery) for about 10 minutes. Add the tomato paste, tomatoes (crushed and diced, including the liquid), and stock and simmer for at least 40 minutes over low heat, stirring occasionally.

6. Stir in the brown sugar and vinegar and simmer for another 20 minutes. Remove from the heat and season with salt, pepper, and the lemon juice.

7. Preheat the oven to 375°F. Put a generous spoonful of filling in the first third of each cabbage leaf. Fold the sides of each leaf in and roll it up as tight as you can. Place the stuffed leaves, seam side down, in a large baking dish, arranging them snugly.

1 large head of green cabbage

Sour cream, for serving

FOR THE FILLING

2 tablespoons each of butter and canola oil

1 pound mushrooms, a few shiitakes would be nice, the rest can be button (caps and stems)

1 medium onion, peeled and diced

1 pound ground turkey

1 red bell pepper, seeded and diced

1 cup cooked barley

1 cup feta cheese

¼ cup chopped fresh dill, or 1 tablespoon dried dill

1 tablespoon sweet Hungarian paprika

1 teaspoon kosher salt

½ teaspoon freshly ground pepper

2 eggs, beaten

FOR THE SAUCE

2 tablespoons each of butter and olive oil

1 medium onion, peeled and diced

1 carrot, peeled and diced

3 stalks celery, split and sliced

3 ounces tomato paste

1 can (28 ounces) whole plum tomatoes, crushed with your fingers

8. Pour the sauce over the cabbage rolls and cover the baking dish with foil. Bake for at least an hour, or until the cabbage leaves are tender to the prick of a fork and the sauce is bubbling. This could take an hour and a half.

9. Carefully, using tongs or a large spatula, place the rolls and sauce on a platter. Serve sour cream on the side.

Wine Tip: German Riesling is our first thought, but if you have a wine seller who is knowledgeable about Austrian wines, this is surely the time to try some.

1 can (28 ounces) diced tomatoes

1 cup chicken stock or vegetable broth

1/2 cup brown sugar

1/2 cup malt vinegar

Kosher salt and ground white pepper to taste

Juice of 1 lemon

Spaetzle

Germans, Hungarians, and Austrians all love their spaetzle—tiny dumplings whose name, translated from German, means "little sparrow." These dumplings are very homey and delicious, the perfect side dish for a variety of hearty entrees. Cookware shops offer a convenient, inexpensive contraption for spaetzle-making; it's basically a hopper that you fill with the dough and slide over a metal panel with holes in it. If you find you like this dish, it's an investment well worth making, even if you use it only a few times a year.

1. Using a large wooden spoon, mix the flour with the eggs, milk, 1/2 teaspoon salt, and baking powder in a large mixing bowl. Stir until the batter is smooth. Set aside.

2. Over medium heat, melt the butter in a double boiler.

3. Bring the water and 1 1/2 tablespoons salt to a boil in a large pot. If you have a spaetzle maker, fill the hopper with the dough and slide it back and forth over the openings at the bottom to shape the dumplings. If you don't, drop the dough into the boiling water a teaspoonful at a time. When the dumplings rise to the surface, test to make sure they are cooked through. Remove them from the boiling water with a slotted spoon and add them to the melted butter. Add the chopped parsley or chives. Gently toss with two forks and keep warm over low heat until serving time.

FOR THE DOUGH

3 cups all-purpose flour

3 eggs

3/4 cup milk

1/2 teaspoon kosher salt

3/4 teaspoon baking powder

3/4 cup (1 1/2 sticks) butter

4 quarts water

1 1/2 tablespoons kosher salt

3 to 4 tablespoons finely chopped fresh parsley or chives (or a combination)

Company Meat Loaf

This "fancy" meat loaf is perfect Big Platter food. It can be made hours ahead and served at room temperature. You can even make it a day ahead and serve it cold. People always "oh and ah" over the hidden egg, as if getting it inside the meat loaf were a magical feat.

1. Preheat the oven to 350°F. In a large bowl, lightly beat the two eggs. Mix in the tomato sauce. Add the ground beef, breadcrumbs, salt, and pepper, and mix, using your hands.

2. Place one-half of the meat mixture on a baking sheet with sides. Form it into a rectangle approximately 8 by 12 inches. Add one-half of the chopped parsley on top of the layer of meat loaf. Sprinkle approximately 1 cup of the shredded mozzarella over the parsley. Place the 2 hard-boiled eggs on top of the cheese.

3. On top of a piece of wax paper, form the remaining meat mixture into a matching rectangle. Add the remaining chopped parsley and mozzarella cheese on top of the second layer of meat loaf. Using your finger, make a groove around the outside edge of the first layer of meat loaf. Flip the second layer on top of the first and press the outside edges to form a seal, stuffing any cheese or parsley that has fallen out back between the two layers. Using the palms of your hands, gently press the top layer so it forms an even mound (this insures more even cooking). With a sharp knife, gently score the top of the loaf in a diamond pattern.

4. Place the meat loaf in the oven for 1 hour. To make the glaze, mix the creamy Italian dressing and mustard together. Remove the meat loaf from the oven. Spoon the glaze over the meat loaf and return it to the oven for an additional 20 minutes. Let the meat loaf stand for 15 minutes before you slice it. Serve it with the Lulu's Root Bake (page 29), along with a green salad with apples and pecans.

Wine Tip: Like most wine-lovers, we're crazy for the Shiraz from Australia, and that's what I'd open to go with this comfort food meal. But meat loaf is an American dish and so you can go with a California Merlot if you want to stay in the U.S.A.

2 eggs

1 can (8 ounces) tomato sauce

3 pounds lean ground beef

1½ cups Italian seasoned breadcrumbs

1 teaspoon kosher salt

½ teaspoon freshly ground pepper

1 bunch parsley, leaves only, finely chopped

2 cups shredded mozzarella cheese

2 hard-boiled eggs, peeled

¼ cup each of creamy Italian dressing and Dijon mustard

Tuna Noodle Casserole, Redux

We once had a tuna noodle casserole cook-off, where everyone made their own version for a Sunday supper. This recipe won the prize for turning a humble housewife's staple from the 1960s into a modern classic. It also won the most expensive casserole award. Tuna steaks aren't in the same price category as the canned variety, but they are worth every penny.

1½ pounds fettuccine

1 tablespoon vegetable oil

3 tablespoons butter

1 pound white button mushrooms, caps and stems, sliced

Kosher salt and freshly ground pepper to taste

3 tablespoons flour

2 cups each of chicken stock and half-and-half or heavy cream

3 pounds fresh tuna steaks

Olive oil, for the tuna (optional)

1 cup lightly toasted pine nuts (see Note)

1 package (10 ounces) frozen peas, or 1 cup fresh snow peas, blanched

1 cup calamata olives, pitted and sliced

1 cup crumbled blue cheese, such as Gorgonzola

¼ cup chopped fresh parsley

1. Prepare the fettuccine according to package directions. Drain and pour into a large bowl. Toss with the oil so the pasta will not stick together. Cover the bowl until the pasta is needed.

2. Melt the butter in a large skillet over medium-high heat. Add the sliced mushrooms, sprinkle with salt and pepper, and sauté until just soft. Reduce heat. Add the flour and blend into a smooth paste around the mushrooms. Allow the mushrooms, butter, and flour mixture to cook slowly for 5 minutes. Stir in the chicken stock and half-and-half and simmer until the mixture thickens, 5 to 7 minutes.

3. There are two ways to deal with the tuna. If you like it rare, smear it with some good olive oil, salt, and pepper and sear in a hot, dry sauté pan or on a stovetop grill, 3 minutes a side, or a couple of minutes more if the steaks are really thick. Set aside until the sauce is done. If you want well-done tuna, just cut it into 1-inch chunks and slip it in the sauce. It will take only about 10 minutes to cook.

4. To the mushroom sauce, add the pine nuts, peas, olives, blue cheese, and if you are making the well-done tuna version, the tuna chunks. Stir over medium heat until the sauce begins to bubble.

5. Put the cooked pasta on a large heated platter. Pour the hot sauce over the pasta, and if you are doing the rare tuna version, cut the tuna into ¼-inch slices then arrange them, overlapping, on top of the pasta. Sprinkle with chopped parsley and serve immediately.

Note: To toast the pine nuts, preheat the oven to 350°F. Place the pine nuts in a single layer on an ungreased baking sheet with sides, and cook for 8 to 10 minutes. Watch carefully, as pine nuts go from nicely toasted to burnt in a matter of moments. Remove the pine nuts from the oven and place in a bowl until needed.

Wine Tip: Tuna and Gorgonzola cheese are two strong tastes. Something red and Italian—Chianti Classico—comes to mind, or maybe something from southern Italy. Mastroberardino is a producer who still cultivates wine varietals the Greeks brought to the Italian peninsula. Try the Greco di Tufo.

Italian Vegetarian

How many of us have found ourselves with vegetarian teenagers or friends who have adopted this lifestyle? Luckily, this doesn't mean you can't produce a delicious special occasion meal. The meat eaters won't even miss meat with all the great flavors in this Italian-inspired menu.

§ **Eggplant Roll-Ups with Caramelized Onions**

§ **Butternut Squash Risotto**

§ **Lulu's Panzanella**

§ **Arugula and Parmesan salad**

§ **Good Italian bread**

§ **Baked Pears with Mascarpone and Amaretti (page 180)**

Wine Tip: We'd have bottles of both white and red Italian open and on the table. The squash risotto would be good with a Tocai from Fruili, and a Barbera from Alba or Asti would be great with the eggplant. Barberas have an acidity that balances red sauce to a tee.

Eggplant Roll-Ups with Caramelized Onions

This is an excellent party dish for an all-vegetarian menu like this one, or for any time there are vegetarians in the crowd. And we won't tell if you use canned sauce, although making a big batch of red sauce and freezing it in Ziploc bags is always a good idea. Of course you can omit the hazelnuts or substitute walnuts or pine nuts, but the flavor and crunch of the hazelnuts are a wonderful surprise.

1. Preheat the oven to 350°F. Soften the eggplant slices by placing them on a baking sheet and roasting for 4 to 5 minutes. Cool them while you make the filling.

2. Combine the three cheeses, eggs, caramelized onions, basil, toasted hazelnuts, and salt and pepper. If you don't have time to caramelize the onions, sauté a diced medium onion and use that.

3. Add about 2 tablespoons of the cheese filling to each of the eggplant slices and roll them up.

4. Place the roll-ups in a greased baking dish with the sides touching. Bake for about 30 minutes at 350°F, until the eggs and cheese are set. Meanwhile, heat the marinara sauce in a separate saucepan.

5. Place the hot roll-ups on an oblong platter and cover them with the sauce.

2 large eggplants, cut the long way into ¼-inch slices

1 pound ricotta cheese

½ cup each of grated Parmesan cheese and shredded mozzarella cheese

2 eggs, beaten

½ cup Caramelized Onions (recipe follows)

¼ cup chopped fresh basil or parsley

¼ cup toasted hazelnuts, coarsely chopped (see Note, page 18)

Kosher salt and freshly ground pepper

Butter, for the baking pan

1 recipe Marinara Sauce (recipe follows), or 1 jar (26 ounces) marinara sauce

Caramelized Onions

3 tablespoons each of butter and olive oil

4 to 6 large sweet onions, peeled, halved, and thinly sliced

1 tablespoon each of kosher salt and sugar

1. In a large sauté pan, heat the butter and olive oil.

2. Sauté the onions over low heat, turning occasionally to coat them with fat, until the onions start to turn translucent, about 10 minutes.

3. Add the salt and sugar and continue to cook over low heat for about an hour, stirring every 10 minutes or so. When done, the onions should be the color of caramel sauce; it may take a few more minutes to get there. Just remember, the patience pays off, and you can watch television while the onions cook, or do the laundry if you must. The onions will last 5 days if refrigerated.

Variation: To make a Moroccan-accented onion compote, stir in ½ cup raisins, ¼ teaspoon cayenne, and a dash of cinnamon during the last few minutes of cooking.

Marinara Sauce

2 tablespoons olive oil

½ cup each of peeled and diced onion, carrot, and celery

6 cloves garlic, peeled and minced

2 large cans (28 ounces each) Italian plum tomatoes

1 small can (8 ounces) tomato paste

2 cups vegetable stock, or chicken stock if you don't need to stay vegetarian

1 cup red wine, more as needed

¼ cup chopped basil leaves

1 teaspoon dried oregano

2 bay leaves

1 tablespoon sugar

Kosher salt and freshly ground pepper to taste

1. Heat the oil in a Dutch oven or heavy stockpot over medium heat.

2. Sauté the mirepoix. When the carrots are soft, about 12 minutes, lower the heat and add the garlic.

3. When the garlic starts to brown (be careful to keep the heat low because garlic can burn so fast), add all the other ingredients, except the black pepper. Crush the tomatoes with your hand or a spoon.

4. Simmer for an hour or two, stirring often; the sugar in the tomatoes can cause them to stick to the bottom of the pan. Add a little more stock or wine as needed. Season with pepper.

5. Cool and chill. We like our sauce chunky but you can use an immersion blender to make it smooth. Pour the sauce over the eggplant roll-ups or freeze it in Ziploc bags for future use.

Butternut Squash **Risotto**

Risotto isn't the first thing you think of as a make-ahead dish. But it is a great Big Platter dish, and you can make it easy to serve by practicing "risotto *interruptus.*" Start your risotto early in the day, take it off the heat when the rice is still crunchy, and spread it out on a baking sheet. Cover the rice with plastic wrap and store it in a cool place or refrigerate. At serving time, heat the remaining wine or stock in your Dutch oven and put the rice in the hot broth. Finish cooking the risotto until the rice is firm but not crunchy. Add the cheese and butter. This method should only take about 15 minutes near party time.

1. Split the squash in half and remove the seeds. Preheat the oven to 400°F. Place the squash, split side down, on a baking sheet that has been sprayed with nonstick baking spray. Roast the squash for about 30 minutes, until it is tender to a fork prick. Cool it, remove the skin, and stir the squash until smooth.

2. Heat the wine or stock to a simmer in a saucepan so you won't be adding cold liquid to the rice. (The principle is to add hot liquids to hot, cold to cold.)

3. In a heavy Dutch oven or large sauté pan, heat the olive oil and 2 tablespoons of the butter over low heat. When the butter is melted, add the onion and sauté it until it turns translucent, about 10 minutes. Add the rice and toss so the kernels are thoroughly coated.

4. With a soup ladle, add the hot liquid to the rice just to cover, stirring as you go. As the liquid is absorbed, add more, a little at a time. Keep the heat low. When the rice is beginning to soften, after about 20 minutes, add the squash puree. When the rice is still al dente but edible, add the cheese and remaining 2 tablespoons butter to finish. The risotto should still be soupy, as it will continue to absorb moisture once off the heat.

5. Serve on a big platter with a lip and throw some Italian parsley leaves and toasted pumpkin seeds on top for garnish.

1 medium butternut squash

Nonstick baking spray

2 quarts white wine, vegetable stock, or a combination (you can substitute chicken stock for a nonvegetarian dish)

2 tablespoons olive oil

¼ cup (½ stick) butter

1 medium onion, peeled and diced

2 cups Arborio rice

½ cup grated Parmesan cheese

Italian (flat-leaf) parsley, for garnish

Toasted pumpkin seeds, for garnish

Lulu's Panzanella

Lulu is squeamish about the more traditional Italian bread salad—where the bread is moistened to a mushy texture. So, in our panzanella, the bread gets toasted before it's added to the juicy vegetables, and then the oil and vinegar is added to the bowl. This is a Dagwood-sandwich kind of a salad—a great way to use up some leftover roast chicken or steak, or the other options listed below. And it is a wonderful way to use summer produce. It needs to sit for a while to really taste good, so you can cover it and put it on the table to rest, adding more dressing right before you eat.

1 loaf day-old French or Italian bread, cut into large pieces and lightly toasted

10 Roma tomatoes, split and sliced, or 6 home-grown tomatoes, diced

2 red onions, peeled, halved, and sliced

1 cup julienned basil leaves

1 cup calamata olives, pitted and drained

1 cup walnuts, lightly toasted (see Note, page 48)

1 cucumber, halved, seeded, and sliced

1 each red and green bell peppers, seeded, quartered, and sliced

1 cup cubed good Parmesan cheese, or 1 cup crumbled Gorgonzola cheese

Optional toppings: 1 cup cooked white beans; 1 cup diced capocollo ham; 1 cup sliced salami; one 8- to 10-ounce tuna fillet, grilled and cubed; 1 small raw zucchini or summer squash, sliced thin

FOR THE VINAIGRETTE

4 cloves garlic, minced, or 6 to 8 roasted cloves garlic, peeled and mashed with a fork

Red wine vinegar and extra-virgin olive oil to taste

Kosher salt and freshly ground pepper to taste

1. Preheat the oven to 325°F. Split a loaf of day-old Italian or French bread in half lengthwise, then halve each of these pieces lengthwise. Cut the pieces into 2-inch-long chunks, place them in a large bowl, and toss them with a drizzle of olive oil. Place on a baking sheet and toast for 10 minutes. The bread will most likely not be browned, but it will have a crusty exterior.

2. Layer all the ingredients, including the optional toppings of your choice, in a large glass bowl or on a platter with a lip. To dress the salad, season it with salt and pepper and douse it with the oil and vinegar to taste. Let it rest for 1 to 1½ hours, then add more oil and vinegar just before serving, as by then the liquids will be absorbed by the bread.

Big Beefsteak Dinner with Three Toppings

When we say "big," we mean BIG. We're talking about either a whole beef tenderloin, usually between 5 and 6 pounds, or a whole New York strip (called "Kansas City strip" in the Midwest), which weighs a whopping 12 to 15 pounds. It's a shame so many people are intimidated by the sheer size of these cuts of meat because not only are they delicious, they practically cook themselves. Although both cuts could be cooked in the oven, they lend themselves beautifully to the grill. Here they are grilled whole and then sliced into steaks in the kitchen.

Traditional wisdom says to count on ½ to ¾ pound of meat per person, but if you know your guests have big appetites, plan on 1 pound for each. That way, you're more likely to be blessed with leftovers. We've offered three different toppings for the steaks—each with the potential to transform a meal into the memorable category. Be sure to serve Wilted Brussels Sprouts with Toasted Walnuts (page 48) on the side. Note: Cooking a cut this large absolutely demands the use of a meat thermometer. Don't attempt to cook these steaks without one, please!

1. Remove the whole steak from the refrigerator about 30 minutes before grilling. Coat all sides of the meat liberally with olive oil (it's easiest to use your hands), then dust with salt and pepper. Insert slivers of fresh garlic into the steak, here and there, if desired.

2. Ignite approximately 3 pounds of charcoal briquettes or an equal amount of lump charcoal, enough to fill a standard chimney-style charcoal starter.

3. Once the coals are covered with light gray ash, divide them equally and push them to opposite sides of the fire grate, leaving the strip in the middle open.

4. If you're grilling a whole tenderloin, start by placing the steak directly over one of the piles of coals. Sear the steak on all sides, a process that should take 6 to 10 minutes. Note: This step is not necessary for the whole New York strip. Once the steak has been seared, place it on the middle of the cooking grate, parallel to the two strips of coals. Place the meat thermometer in either end of the steak, inserting it all the way in. Close the lid, leaving both the top and bottom vents completely open.

5. Turn the tenderloin every 10 to 12 minutes; turn the New York strip every 12 to 15 minutes. Length of cooking time will depend on the size of the steak, the grilling conditions, and how *(continued)*

1 whole beef tenderloin (5 to 6 pounds), or New York strip steak (12 to 15 pounds)

Olive oil

Kosher salt and freshly ground pepper

4 or 5 cloves garlic, peeled and cut into slivers (optional)

well done you want the meat. Begin checking the thermometer on the tenderloin steak after about 20 minutes; begin checking the New York strip after about 40 minutes, remembering in both cases that the internal temperature of the meat increases much faster toward the end of the cooking process than it does in the beginning.

6. Remove the steak when it is 5 to 10 degrees shy of the desired temperature (ultimate temperature for rare is 140°F and 160°F for medium). Transfer the steak to a large cutting board (one that will catch the juices), cover it loosely with foil, and allow the steak to rest for 10 to 15 minutes. Using a large, sharp butcher's knife, carve the steak into slices 1 to 1½ inch thick and serve with one of the following toppings.

Wine Tip: If ever there was a time to enjoy the biggest Cabernet Sauvignon from California that you can afford, this is it. If you are serving the steaks with Southeast Asian "Salsa," you might want a wine with a bit more spice: Shiraz or Zinfandel.

XXX Blue Butter

Linda Scheibal, our friend and one of the best cooks we know, turned us on to this combination. If you're a steak-lover, this topping could become an instant favorite; what's not to like, even if it is a little sinful? As unlikely as it sounds, Cambozola is a German import, which our cheese shop describes as a "blue Brie." And, yes, it's rated "triple cream."

5 ounces Cambozola cheese

5 ounces European-style butter, at room temperature (regular salted butter can be substituted, but for the flavor try to find European butter)

4 to 5 large cloves garlic, pushed through a garlic press

1 tablespoon anchovy paste

Combine all the ingredients in a bowl and mix thoroughly with a fork. Allow the flavors to mellow and combine for an hour before serving. Place about a tablespoon on each hot steak as it is served.

Note: This blue butter can be served as is, right from the bowl or, for a more formal presentation, place the butter on a piece of plastic wrap, shape it into a log-shaped roll, refrigerate, and cut into nice round slices before serving.

Sautéed Mushrooms with Sherry

Mushrooms, sherry, and thyme make a classic combination. As a topping for a steak, it's unbeatable, but it's also great served over polenta for a vegetarian entree.

1. In a large skillet (big enough to accommodate all the mushrooms), melt the butter and olive oil over medium heat. Add the chopped shallots and garlic. Sauté until the shallots start to become transparent, 5 to 6 minutes; do not let them brown.

2. Add the mushrooms, parsley, and thyme. Continue to sauté until the mushrooms release their juices and begin to soften, about 6 minutes.

3. Once the mushrooms are soft, increase the heat, briefly, to high. As the heat increases, add the sherry, stir well, and remove from the stove. Once the mushrooms have cooled a bit, season them with salt and pepper to taste.

2 tablespoons each of butter and extra-virgin olive oil

3 large shallots, peeled and finely minced

3 large cloves garlic, pushed through a garlic press or finely minced

1½ pounds white button mushrooms, caps and stems, sliced

3 tablespoons finely chopped fresh parsley

1 teaspoon fresh thyme, or ½ teaspoon dried thyme

¼ cup medium dry sherry, such as amontillado

¼ teaspoon salt

Freshly ground pepper to taste

Southeast Asian "Salsa"

Our friend Nushi, a great cook who grew up in Iran and subsequently traveled the globe, introduced us to this wham-bang topping for steaks. It originated with her mother, the wife of an ambassador, who knew her way around both the kitchen and the dining room.

Crack the coconut, drain and discard the liquid, and scrape the meat into a blender or food processor fitted with the metal blade. Add the remaining ingredients and process just until combined. Pour into a bowl; cover with plastic wrap and refrigerate for 1 hour before using.

1 fresh coconut

1 bunch cilantro, leaves removed and chopped

3 to 5 serrano chiles, depending on your tolerance for heat, seeded and chopped

Juice of 2 fresh limes

2 to 3 cloves garlic, peeled and pushed through a garlic press

Wilted Brussels Sprouts with Toasted Walnuts

Even if you're not a fan of Brussels sprouts, we urge you to at least take a look at this recipe. It's nothing like the boiled or steamed sprouts you may have had in your past. The combination of lightly sautéed Brussels sprout leaves (the leaves will still be bright green when they're done), small bits of salt pork, toasted walnuts, walnut oil, and sherry vinegar is a real winner. To "deconstruct" Brussels sprouts, cut off the bottom of each sprout; you want to cut just past the core that holds the leaves together. Then pull the sprouts apart so you have individual leaves or bunches of the tight interior leaves. Excellent served with Big Beefsteak Dinner, page 45.

1 tablespoon olive oil

6 to 8 thin slices of salt pork, cut into ¼-inch cubes

⅔ cup walnut pieces, toasted and chopped into ¼-inch pieces (see Note)

2 pounds fresh Brussels sprouts, bottom cores cut off, individual leaves pulled apart, rinsed in cold water

2 to 3 tablespoons toasted walnut oil

6 tablespoons sherry vinegar

Kosher salt and freshly ground pepper to taste

1. Heat the oil in a large, heavy skillet over medium heat. Add the salt pork and sauté until lightly browned, 5 to 7 minutes. Using a slotted spoon, remove the salt pork and let it drain on several layers of paper towels. Leave the leftover oil in the skillet.

2. Add the deconstructed Brussels sprouts to the skillet over medium-high heat along with the salt pork and walnuts. Sauté until the leaves just turn bright green, 5 to 7 minutes.

3. Immediately pour the toasted walnut oil and sherry vinegar over all and sauté about 2 minutes longer. Do not overcook. Add salt and pepper to taste and serve immediately, or at room temperature.

Note: Preheat a toaster oven to 300°F. Spread the walnuts on the baking tray in an even layer. Bake until lightly toasted, 7 to 10 minutes. Note: Walnuts may also be toasted in a dry skillet over medium heat for about 5 minutes.

Pheasant Pot Pie

Growing up in Kansas, Lulu slowly learned to appreciate game, and we both love pheasant, but it has always been a challenge to cook it before it becomes dry and stringy. We've benefited from the counsel of Lulu's son Jed, an excellent game cooker who makes a stroganoff-type dish with pheasant that served as the basis for this elegant pot pie. With this dish, practice has made something like perfect.

1. Heat the butter and oil in a Dutch oven or large, heavy saucepan. Sauté the mushrooms and shallots over medium heat until the mushrooms are soft, about 10 minutes.

2. Sprinkle the mushroom mixture with the flour and stir to form a roux (butter-flour paste). Reduce the heat to low and let the mushroom mixture simmer for 5 minutes so you won't have a raw flour taste in your finished product. Add the parsnips, stock, wine, and port and incorporate the liquids into the mushrooms and roux by stirring for a couple of minutes to make the roux smooth.

3. Let the sauce simmer until the amount of liquid has reduced to about half, stirring occasionally. This should take 30 to 45 minutes.

4. Add the pheasant meat and season with the thyme, salt, and pepper. Cook another 5 minutes, then remove from the heat. Stir in the crème fraîche and peas.

5. Preheat the oven to 350°F. Put the pot pie filling in the casserole dish of your choice; measure the top first to be sure the puff pastry will cover it. Place the pastry on top of the dish, and seal the top of the pie with the pastry.

6. Bake the pot pie until the top is brown and the sides are bubbling. This will take about an hour, depending on the depth of your dish. If you use a standard 9 x 13-inch baking dish, it will most likely take less time.

Note: Cort is a big advocate of pressure cookers though Lulu still has that common childhood fear of them. But if you have one and love it, use it to cook your pheasants, as they stay very moist in this contraption. Cook one pheasant at a time in the pressure cooker. Cort cooks them in a mixture of equal parts chicken stock and dry white wine, 1½ cups to 2 cups total liquid, for 20 to 25 minutes under high pressure. If you don't want to use the pressure cooker method, simmer them in the wine and water until they are tender, about an hour. Check for doneness by trying to pull a little piece of meat off the leg or thigh; it should be tender enough to shred. When cool enough to handle, strip the meat off the birds and shred it using two forks. Reserve the stock to use in the pot pie.

Wine Tip: Choose one of the less expensive Burgundies or an Oregon Pinot. Check your budget and decide—you should cook with the same wine you plan to serve with the dish.

2 tablespoons each of butter and olive oil

1 pound white button mushrooms, caps and stems, sliced

3 shallots, peeled and sliced

2 tablespoons flour

2 parsnips, peeled and diced

2 cups pheasant stock

1 bottle (750 ml) Pinot Noir (see Wine Tip)

4 to 6 ounces port, not the 20-year-old stuff, but not a screw-top variety either

2 to 3 cooked pheasants (about 5 pounds total), meat removed (see Note)

¼ cup fresh thyme leaves

Kosher salt and ground white pepper to taste

1 cup crème fraîche or sour cream

1 package (10 ounces) frozen peas, defrosted

1 sheet frozen puff pastry, defrosted for 10 minutes

In the Spirit of Morocco

The spices and dried fruit used in this salute to Moroccan cooking give familiar ingredients like chicken a new lease on life. And you'll find yourself using the grain pilaf as an accompaniment to all kinds of braised meats and poultry.

§ **Moroccan Chicken**

§ **Couscous and Barley Pilaf**

§ **Lamb Tagine with Prunes and Onion Compote**

§ **Salad with red onions and oranges**

§ **Warm pita bread**

§ **Plum Clafouti (page 174)**

Wine Tip: Spain is the closest wine region to Morocco, so try the luscious Albariño (a white) or a red from the Rioja region.

Moroccan Chicken

This recipe easily expands or contracts depending on the size of the crowd you're serving. For the record, 1½ cups each of apricot nectar and white wine will cover 8 servings of chicken. If you're not a fan of dark meat, use bone-in chicken breasts, one-half breast per person. If you're in a hurry, you can use boneless, skinless chicken breasts but reduce the baking time accordingly.

4 pounds chicken legs and thighs, at least 1 leg and 1 thigh per person

½ teaspoon ground cumin

Kosher salt and freshly ground pepper to taste

1½ cups each of apricot nectar and dry white wine

1 can (15 ounces) garbanzo beans, drained

8 ounces dried apricots

1 stick cinnamon

1 cup lightly toasted almonds (see Note)

1. Preheat the oven to 350°F. Rinse the chicken parts in cold water and pat them dry with paper towels.

2. Place the chicken parts in a deep roasting pan and sprinkle them with the cumin and salt and pepper. Pour equal amounts apricot nectar and wine over the chicken, enough to barely cover the legs and thighs. Add the garbanzo beans, dried apricots, and cinnamon stick and bake, uncovered, for 1½ hours. Baste the chicken with the liquid every 30 minutes or so. If needed, add more of the apricot nectar-wine combination to keep the chicken partially covered in liquid.

3. After 1½ hours, turn the chicken to brown on the other side. Add the almonds and bake for another 30 minutes. Serve with Couscous and Barley Pilaf (page 52).

Note: To toast the almonds, preheat the oven to 325°F. Spread the almonds on a baking sheet and toast them for approximately 15 minutes, until they are lightly browned. Check them every 5 minutes and stir the almonds once.

Couscous and Barley Pilaf

Although this recipe calls for dates and raisins, any dried fruit will do, including apricots, prunes, and cranberries. This makes a wonderful vegetarian main dish served along with some grilled vegetables and a big salad. In that case, you may wish to add ½ teaspoon each of ground cumin and cayenne, plus a scant ¼ teaspoon cinnamon. Otherwise the dish is fairly neutral, depending primarily on the sauce of the chicken or lamb for its flavor. Note: If you have trouble finding uncooked soybeans, check your local health food store.

1½ cups each of uncooked couscous, barley, and soybeans

½ cup each of dried dates, chopped, and golden raisins (plus more of both for garnish)

Kosher salt and ground white pepper to taste

½ cup chopped fresh cilantro leaves, plus additional for garnish

1. Prepare the couscous, barley, and soybeans in separate pans, according to package directions. Drain and rinse the barley and soybeans.

2. Place the cooked couscous, barley, and soybeans in a large bowl. Add the dried fruits, salt, pepper, and cilantro. Toss well.

3. Mound on a platter and garnish with extra dried fruit and cilantro, if desired. You can replace the cilantro with parsley if you are one of the "I hate cilantro" bunch.

Lamb Tagine with Prunes and Onion Compote

Moroccan stews, called tagines, are just the thing for entertaining. They are flavorful and need long cooking, so you can start the process well before the first guest arrives.

1. In a large, heavy ovenproof saucepan, melt the butter and olive oil over medium-high heat. Add the sliced onions and sauté until just wilted. Add the ginger and garlic slices and sauté a few minutes longer. Add the cubed lamb to the pan, stirring occasionally until the lamb is browned.

2. Meanwhile, in a small sauté pan over low heat, combine the dry spices, heat them until you start to smell their aromas, and remove from the heat. Try not to inhale over the pan as it is hard on the lungs. Sprinkle the toasted spices over the lamb and continue browning for another 5 minutes.

3. Add water to cover the lamb, about 4 cups. Cover and simmer for 1 hour, stirring occasionally and adding more water if necessary. After an hour, add the prunes and more water (about 2 cups) and simmer for another 40 minutes or so. If you want to cook this dish in the oven, after you've browned the meat and added the spices and water, put the saucepan in a preheated 375°F oven, cover, and cook for 1 hour. Add the prunes and check for tenderness every 30 minutes or so, stirring as you do.

4. If possible, make this dish the morning or the night before serving and let it set for the flavors to marry. Reheat at dinnertime, adjusting the salt. Transfer the tagine to a large platter with a lip and top with the onion compote.

2 tablespoons each of butter and olive oil

2 medium yellow onions, peeled and thinly sliced

3-inch piece of fresh ginger, peeled and cut into ½-inch slices

4 to 6 cloves garlic, peeled and thinly sliced

5-pound boneless leg of lamb, cut into 1½-inch cubes

4 whole cloves

2 teaspoons kosher salt

1 teaspoon freshly ground pepper

2 teaspoons crushed red pepper flakes

1 teaspoon each of ground cinnamon and cumin

½ teaspoon ground cardamom

¼ teaspoon ground nutmeg

1½ cups pitted prunes

1 recipe Caramelized Onions (see Variation, page 40)

Cowboy Cassoulet

If you have ever read any French regional cookbook, you will know there is a great deal of controversy over the various recipes for cassoulet. Each town in southwestern France has its own version. So we created a version with an eye on Texas. We figured a Texas cassoulet would have beef as the main ingredient—a choice that seemed just as valid as the other ingredients deemed necessary for a real cassoulet. This one fulfills the only truly necessary requirement in our book: it tastes delicious.

Cowboy Cassoulet can be prepared over a two- or three-day period. The beans can be cooked and the meat roasted one or two days ahead of time, then the dish can be completed the day you are presenting it. Although there are several steps, none of them are difficult.

---

5 pounds trimmed beef stew meat

Kosher salt and freshly ground pepper to taste

2 cinnamon sticks

4 to 5 cloves garlic, peeled and minced

2 to 4 dried ancho chiles, soaked in warm water for at least 30 minutes

2 pounds dried Great Northern beans

3 pounds hot or mild Italian sausages

6 tablespoons butter

2 tablespoons olive oil

2 yellow onions, peeled and finely diced

2 large carrots, peeled and finely diced

4 stalks celery, finely diced

1 can (28 ounces) tomatoes, diced

Chicken stock, up to 2 quarts

2 to 3 cups fresh breadcrumbs, depending on the surface of your baking dish (see Note)

1 cup chopped fresh parsley

1. Preheat the oven to 375°F. In a large roasting pan, toss the meat with salt and pepper, add the cinnamon sticks, garlic, and chiles with their soaking water. Cover and roast for 2 to 3 hours, until the meat is tender. Cool and refrigerate, removing the congealed fat before you proceed to the final step.

2. Meanwhile, soak the dried beans in water that covers them by 2 inches for at least 2 hours. Add more water to maintain the water level; the beans will absorb moisture as they soak. Bring to a boil, then reduce the heat and simmer the beans until tender, about 1 hour, adding salt to taste. Transfer the beans to a storage container and cool them completely by surrounding the container with an ice water bath. Refrigerate them until you are ready to finish the cassoulet.

3. Preheat the oven to 375°F. Prick the sausage every 3 or 4 inches on both sides and roast them on a baking sheet with a lip for 25 minutes. Cool the sausages and cut them into 3-inch chunks. (Why cut them after cooking instead of before? Because you won't lose all those good juices.) If you cook the sausages just before you are going to finish the cassoulet, just set them aside. If you cook the sausages the night before, cover them and refrigerate.

4. Heat 2 tablespoons of the butter and the oil in a skillet and sauté the mirepoix (onions, carrots, and celery) over medium heat until the onions are translucent, about 10 minutes. Remove from the heat.

5. In a large roasting pan or cazuela (see page 187), combine the beef, beans, sausage, and mirepoix. Include the ancho chiles as well, but if they were destroyed while roasting in step 1, soak two more for 20 minutes and add them and their soaking water. Add the diced tomatoes and mash them further with your hand. (You can do this the morning of the party, if that will help you timewise. Just wait to add the stock.)

6. Preheat the oven to 350°F. Add enough homemade or canned chicken stock to the cassoulet to make the whole mixture very wet. At this point, the stock should very slightly cover the bean-meat mixture.

7. Melt the 4 remaining tablespoons butter in a large saucepan. Remove the pan from the heat, add the breadcrumbs and parsley, and toss. Place the breadcrumb mixture gently over the cassoulet.

8. Bake until the sides are bubbling, the crumbs are browned, and the middle of the cassoulet is hot. Depending on the depth of your pan, this could take 1 to 1½ hours. Serve in the casserole. If you wish, discard the ancho chiles and cinnamon stick before serving. We don't take them out; it disturbs the crust of the dish.

Note: When we have a good hunk of dry bread left—French, sourdough, something with some guts—we stick it in the freezer in a storage bag. When we have three or four of these, we make breadcrumbs. Let the bread thaw, chop it into large pieces by splitting the loaves down the middle, then slicing them every 3 or 4 inches. Put this bread on baking sheets and lightly toast it at 325°F for 15 minutes, give or take. Let the bread cool and then put it in the food processor a few pieces at a time and pulverize. Transfer to a Ziploc bag, and store in the freezer. That said, using commercial breadcrumbs or those from your local bakery will not ruin your cassoulet.

Wine Tip: We turn again to Beaujolais, which we know will be a steadfast friend to this dish. We've also served it with a red Rhône, Vieux Telegraphe, delicious if you want to splurge a bit.

Pear, Beet, Shrimp, and Goat Cheese Salad

This is a great whole-meal salad or a wonderful addition to the buffet table. It serves 8 to 15 depending on the rest of the menu. You can make it without the shrimp if you desire.

6 whole red beets, unpeeled

3 whole yellow beets, unpeeled (if yellow beets are unavailable, use more red beets)

1 pound arugula, or a mixture of spinach and arugula

2½ pounds medium-sized (20-count) precooked shrimp (4 to 6 shrimp per person), plus 6 more for garnish

3 ripe pears

Kosher salt to taste, plus ½ teaspoon for the dressing

1 tablespoon olive oil

3 tablespoons vinegar (your choice of red wine, sherry, or balsamic)

⅔ cup toasted pine nuts (see Note, page 38)

¼ cup extra-virgin olive oil

Freshly ground pepper to taste

5½ ounces mild goat cheese

1. Cut the tops off the beets, leaving approximately ½ inch of the stems intact. This will keep the beets from bleeding as they cook. If you're using both red and yellow beets, cook them in separate pots.

2. Put the beets in a large saucepan; cover with cold water. Cook the beets over high heat for about 45 minutes, until they can be easily pierced with a fork at their thickest point. Drain and immediately submerge them in cold water for approximately 15 minutes. This will stop the cooking process and makes the beets so easy to peel, the skins will slip off in your hands. Place the peeled beets in a plastic bag and chill thoroughly, about 1 hour. Note: This step can be done the night before the salad is to be served.

3. After cooking, cut 3 red beets in half lengthwise, then into ⅜-inch slices. Place in a large salad bowl. Top with the arugula. Place the shrimp on top of the arugula, reserving 6 for garnish. Slice and core (but do not peel) the pears into ⅜-inch slices, reserving 1 for garnish. Add the pears to the top of the salad. (The beets will color the pears so keep them separated for as long as possible.) Cut the remaining beets (red and, if using, yellow) into ⅜-inch-thick rounds. Place them in a medium-sized bowl, toss with kosher salt to taste, and drizzle with the olive oil and 1 tablespoon of the vinegar. Using your hands, gently toss to coat the beets evenly with the dressing.

4. Arrange the dressed red and yellow beets around the edge of a large, flat-edged platter, alternating red and yellow rounds. Add ⅓ cup toasted pine nuts to the salad, reserving ⅓ cup for garnish.

5. To prepare the dressing, dissolve the ½ teaspoon kosher salt in the remaining vinegar in a small bowl. Sprinkle the salt-vinegar mixture over the salad. Drizzle the olive oil over the salad and toss gently. Once evenly coated, add a generous grind of pepper to taste and pile the salad into the middle of the beet-ringed platter. Crumble goat cheese on top. Garnish with reserved pine nuts, shrimp, and pear slices.

Wine Tip: Shrimp and Chardonnay are one of those magic combinations. Sauvignon Blanc and goat cheese are another. Either varietal will strike a note of companionship somewhere on your palate.

Spicy Hacked **Chicken**

We always had a whole roasted chicken on the menu at Cafe Lulu, and this spicy hacked-up version was a favorite of our guests. We love watching skilled Asian cooks hack up a chicken. Although you may not cut across the bird with the finesse that long experience provides, it is fun to carve a chicken in a different way. And the spicy taste of the skin is wonderful, no matter how you slice it.

1. Preheat the oven to 400°F. Rinse the chickens, removing the neck, gizzard, and other innards, and pat them dry with paper towels. Place the chickens breast side up on a rack in a shallow baking dish and roast for 30 minutes. This process crisps the skin so it won't stick to the foil in the following step.

2. Remove the chickens from the oven. Reduce the temperature to 350°F. Combine all the sauce ingredients in a large bowl. Spoon about ¼ cup of the sauce into each of the chickens' cavities. Liberally baste the outside of the chickens with more of the sauce. Return the chickens to the baking dish and cover with foil. Bake for 1 hour. Remove the birds and baste again. Bake for an additional 20 minutes, uncovered, basting the chickens often. Many of the ingredients in the sauce contain sugar; as it caramelizes, the chickens will turn a dark mahogany color. Don't worry if parts of the skin blacken; it won't hurt the flavor of this dish.

3. Remove the chickens from the oven to rest. Meanwhile, place any remaining sauce in a small pan and bring it to a boil. Reduce the heat to low and simmer for 5 minutes.

4. Now for the "hacking" process. Using a large butcher knife or Chinese cleaver, cut the chickens in half, the opposite way from what you're probably used to doing. Starting in the middle, cut the chickens in half from leg to leg. Cut each piece in half again. Arrange on a platter, garnish with the cilantro, basil, and sesame seeds, and serve the warm sauce on the side.

Wine Tip: Alsace Gewürztraminer has the spiciness to match this dish.

2 whole large frying chickens (4 to 5 pounds each)

FOR THE SAUCE
¼ cup sesame oil

½ cup Thai sweet chili sauce

1 cup sherry, dry to medium dry

¼ cup medium-bodied soy sauce, such as Pearl River Soy or the low-salt Kikkoman brand

½ cup chunky peanut butter

¼ cup sriracha chili-garlic sauce

4-inch piece of fresh ginger, minced (about ¼ cup)

FOR THE GARNISH
Fresh cilantro leaves

Purple or green basil leaves, or both

Black sesame seeds

The end of summer is a busy time in Napa Valley. There are thousands of acres of grapes to be picked and crushed, and the predominantly Hispanic vineyard workers are hard at it from daybreak to sundown in 100-degree-plus temperatures. As a show of appreciation, individual wineries throw an "End-of-Harvest Party." Although our feast doesn't feature a pig cooked in a pit, it does include the crispy, succulent *puerco muerto,* plus some very toothsome additions.

§ **Roasted Pork Shoulder with Squash Puree**

§ **Salmon on Black Beans with Red Pepper Puree**

§ **Turkey Enchilada Pie**

§ **Pumpkin Flan with Sweet Tortilla Chips (page 181)**

Wine Tip: Sparkling or Zinfandel. We love sparkling wine with rich, fatty meats such as pork because the wine cleans the palate as you sip. A lean, mean version, such as Gloria Ferrer, would be our pick. But in honor of the harvest, the wonderful Zinfandels of Northern California should be on the wine menu as well. Or abandon wine altogether in favor of margaritas and plenty of Mexican beer.

Roasted Pork Shoulder with Squash Puree

The centerpiece of Mexican harvest parties here in Napa Valley is pork, usually in the form of *carnitas* ("little meats"), where a whole pig is first cooked, usually underground, and then cut into small pieces and allowed to crisp in a cauldron (yes, a cauldron) of boiling lard. Lard will not boil unless there is some moisture present: some use Coca-Cola, others whole fresh oranges. Still others keep their methods secret. In the end, there are bite-sized pieces of pork (laughingly referred to as *puerco muerto* or "dead pork"), deliciously crisp on the outside and succulent on the inside. This recipe follows a different, easier path but arrives at the same delicious destination.

1. Prepare the marinade the night before cooking. Put the garlic, onion, and ginger in the food processor and add the two kinds of soy sauce, 1/2 cup of the peanut oil, the sesame oil, and the hot sauce. Puree the marinade, transfer to a large storage container (big enough to hold the pork), and stir the sherry, vinegar, and lime juice into the puree.

(continued)

FOR THE MARINADE

10 cloves garlic, smashed with a chef's knife, skins removed

1 onion, peeled and quartered

3-inch piece of ginger, peeled and sliced

1/2 cup each of dark soy sauce or tamari and light soy sauce, such as green-label Kikkoman

¾ **cup peanut or canola oil**

¼ **cup each of sesame oil and Mexican hot sauce (the Crystal or Valentina brands are favorites)**

½ **cup each of dry sherry, malt vinegar, and fresh lime juice**

1 pork shoulder (6 to 7 pounds)

2 quarts white wine, water, or chicken stock, or a combination

1 recipe Pumpkin Seed Sauce (recipe follows)

1 recipe Squash Puree (recipe follows)

2. Put the pork shoulder in the container and marinate overnight, turning the meat over a couple of times. The pork can stay in this mix until you begin the roasting process, which will take 4 to 5 hours, depending on the size of the shoulder.

3. In this case, you don't need to brown the pork because the marinade contains so many things with high sugar content. Hot oil and this marinade could make for burnt skin on the pork and maybe on you. When ready to cook, preheat the oven to 375°F. Put the pork in a large roasting pan, fat side up, with the marinade and a quart of the liquid. Cover the pan and roast for a couple of hours, then turn the roast over, add a little more liquid, cover, and stick back in the oven. Check it every hour, adding more liquid if needed and spooning the juices over the top. When you can pull a piece of meat off easily and it melts in your mouth, you might want to uncover the pork and cook it for another 30 to 45 minutes to crisp it up.

4. Remove the roast from the oven and let it set for 20 minutes.

5. You have to do this part with your hands and maybe a big fork. Pull the meat apart in hunks and pile it on a big platter, leaving room on both ends for the Squash Puree. (Do not, under any circumstances, slice the pork with a knife. Shoulder meat has to be pulled so it retains its muscle integrity, thus the term "pulled pork.") Serve Pumpkin Seed Sauce on the side.

Pumpkin Seed Sauce

3 tablespoons canola oil

½ **cup each of peanuts, pumpkin seeds, and sunflower seeds**

2 cups chicken stock

1 can (28 ounces) diced or crushed tomatoes

1 tablespoon Mexican hot sauce

Kosher salt, if needed

1. In a large, heavy saucepan, heat the oil over medium heat and brown the nuts and seeds, 3 to 5 minutes. When the pumpkin seeds are popping, remove the pan from the heat.

2. Place the toasted nuts and seeds in a food processor, or if you have an immersion blender leave them right in the pan. Add the stock, tomatoes, and hot sauce and emulsify the sauce or puree in the food processor. Taste for salt, but you probably won't need any.

Squash Puree

1. Preheat the oven to 400°F. Split the squash in half and scoop out the seeds.

2. Roast the squash face down on a nonstick baking sheet, or one that you have sprayed with nonstick baking spray, until they are tender when pierced with a fork, about 40 minutes.

3. Remove the squash from the oven and let them cool for 30 minutes or so, lifting them up at some point so the steam in the cavities is released. Take care that you don't burn yourself.

4. Remove the outer peel from the squash. You can prepare the squash to this point early in the day and set aside.

5. When your pork is close to done, heat the half-and-half and butter in a large saucepan, add the squash puree and spices, including salt and white pepper, and mash the mixture as you would mashed potatoes. If you want to do this an hour before your guests arrive, you can put it in an ovenproof pan and stick it in the oven to keep warm. After you remove the pork from the oven, reduce the oven temperature to 200°F until you are ready to present the dish. Put mounds of the squash on either end of the pork platter.

2 acorn and 1 butternut squash (about 5 pounds total)

Nonstick baking spray (if needed)

1 cup half-and-half

¼ cup (½ stick) butter

½ teaspoon each of cinnamon and cardamom

Kosher salt and ground white pepper to taste

Salmon on Black Beans with Red Pepper Puree

This dish was inspired by a meal Cort had at the elegant Heathman Hotel in Portland, Oregon, some twenty years ago. He was dining alone and feeling more than a little adventurous, so he decided to order something he wouldn't ordinarily consider. The combination of salmon and black beans sounded so outlandish that he decided to give it a try. Right then and there he realized that salmon had enough flavor to stand up to other assertive flavors splendidly. Top the dish with red pepper puree, crème fraîche, and a few fresh cilantro leaves, and you have an instant classic and a frequent Big Platter entree.

Nonstick baking spray, for the pan

1 side (fillet) of salmon (about 4 pounds)

1 lime

Vegetable oil

Ground white pepper

Paprika

6 ounces crème fraîche, for garnish

1/4 cup fresh cilantro leaves, for garnish

FOR THE BLACK BEANS

2 tablespoons vegetable oil

2 medium yellow onions, peeled and finely chopped

4 cans (15 ounces each) black beans

2 teaspoons ground cumin

1 teaspoon chili powder

1 can (14 ounces) chicken or vegetable stock

FOR THE RED PEPPER PUREE

3 red bell peppers, seeded and quartered

2 orange bell peppers, seeded and quartered

1/4 cup olive oil

Kosher salt

1. Preheat the oven to 350°F. Spray a baking sheet large enough to handle the salmon with nonstick baking spray.

2. Unwrap the salmon (save the paper wrapping) and rinse it under cold water. Blot dry using several layers of paper towel. Place the salmon on the wrapping paper, skin side down, and squeeze the lime over it. Rub the salmon with an even, light coating of vegetable oil (your hands work best for this job). Dust it lightly with white pepper and paprika. Place the salmon on a greased baking sheet and store in the refrigerator until ready to cook.

3. To make the beans, heat the vegetable oil in a large skillet over medium-high heat. Add the chopped onions and sauté until just soft, about 7 minutes.

4. Drain the black beans and add them to the skillet. Stir in the cumin and chili powder. Cook the beans and onions until thoroughly heated. Using a potato masher, coarsely mash the beans. Remove from the heat and place about 2 cups of the beans in a blender. Blend them, adding as much of the chicken or vegetable stock as necessary to create a smooth puree. Once smooth, return the puree to the black bean mixture in the skillet and mix thoroughly. Set aside.

5. To make the red pepper puree, put the quartered peppers in a baking pan, drizzle with olive oil and sprinkle with salt, cover with foil, and roast in the preheated 350°F oven for 1 hour, until completely wilted and soft. Let the peppers rest for 15 minutes or so, then slip off the skins and put the peppers and the juices from the baking pan into a blender or food processor. Process until smooth, drizzling with more olive oil as you go. Taste and add salt, if necessary. Set aside until needed.

6. Increase the oven temperature to 450°F. Remove the salmon from the refrigerator and place the baking sheet in the oven. Cook for exactly 12 minutes. While the salmon is cooking, reheat the black bean mixture over medium heat. Add more stock if necessary; the beans should be about the consistency of mashed potatoes.

7. Just before the salmon is done, spread the black beans on the bottom of a big platter (big enough for the salmon) in an even layer. With a helper and two spatulas, place the salmon on top of the black beans. Pour the room-temperature red pepper puree over the top of the salmon and dot with teaspoonfuls of crème fraîche and the cilantro leaves, if desired. To serve, cut the salmon across the grain into 1-inch-thick slices, making sure each person gets some black beans, pepper puree, and crème fraîche.

Turkey Enchilada Pie

We first made this dish years ago as a means of using up post-Thanksgiving turkey. For some reason, there always seemed to be more leftover dark meat than light, and this rich, flavorful meat was wonderful with the red enchilada sauce. This is a great party dish, since the appeal of its flavors seems to span all age groups. The following recipe is for a 9 x 13-inch pan; increase the recipe by 50 percent for an 11 x 16-inch pan.

2 tablespoons vegetable oil, plus additional for frying the tortillas

1 yellow onion, peeled and diced

1/2 cup pickled diced jalapeño peppers

4 to 5 cups cooked turkey meat, preferably dark meat, shredded or cut into small cubes

1/4 cup chopped fresh cilantro, plus additional for garnish, if desired

2 cans (28 ounces each) red enchilada sauce

18 corn tortillas (6-inch size)

Nonstick baking spray, for the pan

1 can (6 ounces) pitted black olives, drained

8 ounces Monterey Jack cheese, shredded

Sour cream for garnish, if desired

1. Preheat the oven to 350°F. In a large frying pan, heat the vegetable oil over medium heat and sauté the onion until just soft, about 6 minutes. Add the jalapeño peppers, turkey meat, and cilantro. Cook for 5 minutes, stirring occasionally. Set aside.

2. Pour about 1/2 inch vegetable oil into one medium-sized skillet and the red enchilada sauce into another. Put the stack of tortillas on one side of the stove (right or left, depending on which direction you plan on assembling the ingredients), then the pans of oil and enchilada sauce, each on a burner, and lastly, the baking pan, arranged like an assembly line. Spray the inside of the baking pan with nonstick baking spray. Adjust the heat to medium under the pans of oil and enchilada sauce and have of a pair of tongs at the ready. Test the temperature of the oil by placing an edge of a tortilla into the pan; the oil is hot enough if the tortilla immediately starts to sizzle.

3. Place a tortilla in the hot oil; cook for about 20 seconds per side. Remove the tortilla from the oil with the tongs, allowing excess oil to drip back into the pan. Dip the tortilla into the enchilada sauce and then place it on the bottom of the baking pan.

4. Continue frying and dipping the tortillas and arranging them overlapping by half, to cover the entire bottom of the baking pan; six tortillas should do it. Spread about half the turkey mixture on top of the tortilla layer, dot with olives and half the shredded cheese, and then make another layer of fried-and-dipped tortillas. Follow with another round of the meat, olive, and cheese layers, and a final layer of fried-and-dipped tortillas. Pour the remaining enchilada sauce over the pile and top with a little additional shredded cheese, if desired. Cover the pan with aluminum foil.

5. Bake the enchilada pie for 1 hour; the sauce should be bubbling up the sides of the pan. Cook for an additional 10 to 15 minutes, if necessary. Cut the pie into squares and top with sour cream and chopped cilantro, if desired.

Big Platter Winter

Winter sends us closer to the hearth and even closer to the kitchen. Perfect timing because the winter months, with their multiple holidays, offer plenty of occasions for Big Platter cooking. It's a season when most of us are never quite sure how many guests are going to show up, so it's a great idea to err on the side of "more." After all, generous hospitality plays an important role in the spirit of the season!

Bourbon and Coke Short Ribs

We love short ribs, but so does everyone else who's written a cookbook in this century. Short ribs with corn and plantains? Check. Short ribs braised in beer? Check. The array of available recipes is amazing, and now here's another idea: Lulu's son Jed, who lives in Kentucky, and her daughter Reagan, who writes about food and travel for the *Atlanta Journal-Constitution,* both mentioned Coke as a good braising liquid for short ribs. It was Reagan who said, "Make it Bourbon and Coke Short Ribs, Mom." And so we did, and they are luscious. Short ribs are so much better the second day, so make them ahead, and store the sauce and the ribs separately in the refrigerator. Reheat them the evening of the party, adding more moisture (Coke and stock) if necessary.

1. Preheat the oven to 350°F. In a large, heavy sauté pan, heat the oil, season the short ribs with salt and pepper, and brown all the short ribs, placing them in a large roasting pan as you go.

2. Take a look at your sauté pan and if it doesn't have too many burned bits of meat and fat, you can add the butter and sauté the mirepoix (carrots, onions, and celery) in the same pan. If there's too much burned stuff, start with a clean sauté pan.

3. When the onions start to wilt, add the garlic and cook another 3 minutes. Stir in the soy sauce, Worcestershire sauce, mustard seeds, caraway seeds, and allspice berries, and then put the whole mixture on top of the ribs.

4. Add 2 cups of the chicken stock, 2 cans of the Coke, and ½ cup of the bourbon. Cover and roast at for 2 hours.

5. Turn the ribs carefully so they don't disconnect from the bone. Add the third can of Coke, the remaining bourbon, and 1 cup stock. Bake for another 2 hours. The short ribs are done when the meat is tender and pulls away easily from the bone.

6. Either serve immediately or cool and store the ribs and sauce separately until serving time the next day. The red cabbage recipe on page 71 and the greens recipe on page 87 are great with the ribs.

Wine Tip: A massive California Petite Syrah comes to mind or something from the southern Rhône. Gigondas? Châteauneuf-du-Pape? We've got lots of flavors going here and the richness of the meat itself so this dish needs something big enough to stand up and contribute, not be wimpy.

⅓ cup canola oil

12 large short ribs, or if you're serving more than 8 people, estimate 1½ ribs per person

Kosher salt and freshly ground pepper to taste

2 tablespoons butter

2 carrots, peeled and diced

1 large or 2 medium onions, peeled and diced

3 stalks celery, split and diced

6 cloves garlic, peeled and crushed with the flat side of a cleaver or chef's knife, then diced

1 tablespoon each of soy sauce and Worcestershire sauce

1 teaspoon each of mustard seeds and caraway seeds

½ teaspoon allspice berries

3 cups chicken stock

3 cans Coca-Cola (not diet)

1 cup good bourbon

Abraham Lincoln's Favorite Dinner

We're both lucky enough to have a great friend, Kansas City artist and raconteur, John Puscheck (as he says, "That's ketchup spelled backward," but did we mention John is dyslexic?). When John was a youngster in Indiana, his mother made this dish, which she advertised as "Abraham Lincoln's favorite dinner." John thinks his mother may have been lying, but we think it's comfort food at its best. Make sure you make some cornbread to sop up the juices.

---

4 to 5 pounds smoked pork shanks or ham hocks, each cut into 3 or 4 slices

3 to 4 pounds small new potatoes, skins on

3 pounds string beans, ends snipped off

4 to 6 tablespoons butter

Freshly ground pepper to taste

1 white onion, peeled and diced

1. Place the slices of pork shank in the bottom of a tall stockpot. Add enough cold water to barely cover. Place the new potatoes on top of the pork and the string beans on top of the new potatoes.

2. Bring to a boil over high heat. Cover and reduce the heat to a simmer. Cook for 2 hours.

3. Take the string beans, new potatoes, and pork out of the pot. Reserve the cooking liquid (known as "pot likker" in some parts of the country). Take the meat off the shanks or hocks, trim off the fat, and reserve the meat.

4. Roughly chop the potatoes and spread them in a layer on a large platter. Dot generously with butter and freshly ground pepper. Place the string beans on top of the potato layer and then top with the pork. Drizzle some of the reserved "pot likker" over all and sprinkle with the diced white onion. Everyone should take some of everything, along with a slice or two of cornbread. Good eatin'!

Wine Tip: Wines that go with ham took us back to Italy and another wonderful combination with prosciutto, the Friulian white Tocai. It should do Abe's favorite proud.

Stuffed Shells with Mushroom Sauce

Although pasta seems like a natural Big Platter dish, most pasta recipes require a lot of last-minute preparation. The beauty of this one is you can make the sauce and the filling the day ahead. You can cook the manicotti or shells earlier in the day and even stuff the shells in the morning. Then, at show time, all you have to do is pour the sauce over the filled pastas, bake, and serve.

---

1. To make the mushroom sauce, melt 4 tablespoons of the butter in a large, heavy saucepan over low heat. Add the sliced button mushrooms and sauté until they're soft and all the moisture has been released from the mushrooms and has evaporated.

2. Add the remaining 2 tablespoons butter to the sautéed mushrooms. Allow it to melt over medium heat. Add the flour, stir well, and cook for 5 minutes.

3. Add the porcini mushrooms, along with the water they were soaked in (all but the gritty bits in the bottom of the bowl). Cook for 5 minutes over medium heat. Add the half-and-half, salt, white pepper, and nutmeg. Simmer for 15 to 20 minutes. Add the Parmesan, stir, and cook over low heat for an additional 5 to 10 minutes. The sauce is done when it has thickened slightly.

4. To make the filling, in a mixing bowl, combine the eggs, ricotta, mozzarella, spinach, walnuts, and salt and pepper. Stir in ¾ cup of the Parmesan. Cover and chill until needed.

5. Preheat the oven to 375°F. Meanwhile, cook the manicotti or giant shells for a few minutes less than specified in package directions. Drain, let cool, then fill the shells with the ricotta mixture.

6. Arrange the shells in a casserole or baking dish so they touch but are not crammed in. Pour or spoon the sauce over the shells so they are almost covered. Sprinkle the top of the dish with the remaining ¼ cup Parmesan. Bake until the top is browned and the sauce is bubbling, about 40 minutes.

Wine Tip: Salice Salentino from Dr. Taurino in Italy. We've recommended this in the fall section as well, because it's a great food wine. Or try a Tuscan wine from the recently "hot" region, the Maremma.

1 pound manicotti or giant shells

FOR THE MUSHROOM SAUCE
1 ounce dried porcini mushrooms, soaked in 4 cups warm water for at least 30 minutes

1 pound white button mushrooms, rinsed and sliced

6 tablespoons butter

2 to 3 tablespoons flour

1 pint half-and-half or heavy cream

½ teaspoon kosher salt

Ground white pepper to taste

¼ teaspoon grated nutmeg

½ cup grated Parmesan cheese

FOR THE PASTA FILLING
2 eggs, lightly beaten

1 pound ricotta cheese

1 cup shredded mozzarella cheese

1 package (10 ounces) frozen chopped spinach, defrosted and squeezed to remove excess moisture

1 cup walnuts, toasted and chopped (see Note, page 48)

Kosher salt and freshly ground pepper to taste

1 cup grated Parmesan or Asiago cheese

Corned Beef and White Beans

This is an adaptation of an old French country dish, typically made with corned pork. As corned pork is all but impossible to find in this country, corned beef is a good, and readily available, substitute. Rustic, full flavored, and very satisfying, this is a meal for a cold and blustery night. About all you need to accompany it would be a simple green salad and crusty French bread. This is one of those dishes even better served the second day.

1 pound small dried white beans

5-pound corned beef brisket

2 tablespoons each of vegetable oil and butter

2 large carrots, sliced into rounds

4 stalks celery, sliced

2 large leeks, white part only, washed free of grit and sliced (or substitute 1 large onion, chopped)

2 to 3 cloves garlic, pushed through a garlic press

1/4 cup finely chopped fresh parsley leaves, plus more for garnish

2 quarts cold water

2 cans (14.5 ounces each) stewed tomatoes

2 bay leaves

1 teaspoon each of dried rosemary, dried thyme, dried mustard, and ground pepper

1. Rinse the beans with cold water and place them in a large pot. Add enough water to cover the beans by 3 inches. Bring to a boil over high heat for 1 minute. Remove from the heat, cover, and let stand for 1 hour. Drain the beans and set them aside.

2. To reduce the saltiness of the meat, place the corned beef in a large kettle and cover it with water. Bring to a boil over high heat for 2 minutes. Remove from the heat, drain, and set aside in the kettle.

3. Heat the oil and butter in a large frying pan over medium heat. Add the carrots, celery, leeks, garlic to taste, and parsley. Sauté for approximately 10 minutes, or until just soft.

4. Spoon the vegetables over the corned beef in the kettle. Add the water, stewed tomatoes, bay leaves, rosemary, thyme, dried mustard, and pepper. Add the reserved beans.

5. Bring the corned beef and bean mixture to a boil over high heat. Reduce the heat to low, cover the kettle, and simmer for approximately 3½ hours, or until the meat is very tender and the beans mash easily with a fork.

6. Once the corned beef is cooked, remove it from the kettle, allow it to cool a little, then cut it into large chunks.

7. Skim off any fat that has floated to the surface of the beans. Discard the bay leaves. Spoon out about 2 cups of the bean-vegetable mixture and either puree it in a blender or mash it well with a potato masher. Add it back to the kettle and stir well. Taste and add salt, if needed.

8. Reheat the bean mixture, pour it into a large, deep platter, and top it with the chunks of corned beef. Garnish with additional chopped parsley, if desired.

Wine Tip: As rustic as this is, we'd go with Beaujolais, but we could see French Bordeaux as well, just not a super-expensive bottle.

Red Cabbage and Apples

Everyone of European heritage has a version of sweet and sour cabbage in their family cookbook. We like this one for the special way the burnt sugar and red wine vinegar combine and for the addition of the apples. Don't worry if the sugar hardens when you pour it over the cabbage. The vinegar and the cooking heat will liquefy it again.

2 tablespoons each of butter and olive oil

1 large head red cabbage, thinly sliced

3 Granny Smith apples, cored and thinly sliced, peel on

1 cup sugar

1 cup red wine vinegar

Kosher salt and ground white pepper to taste

1. Melt the butter and oil in a heavy sauté pan over medium heat. Reduce the heat to low and add the sliced cabbage. When the cabbage begins to soften, add the apples. Sauté slowly, stirring frequently, about 20 minutes total.

2. Meanwhile, pour the sugar into a separate heavy saucepan. Place the pan over medium heat and slowly melt the sugar, stirring often as the edges begin to liquefy. When the sugar turns a light brown, add it to the sautéed cabbage and apples. Stir in the vinegar and season with salt and white pepper. Continue to cook until the cabbage and apple slices are caramelized, approximately another 20 minutes. Serve hot or at room temperature.

New Year's Day Pig Party

Several years ago, we threw a memorable New Year's Day pig party with our friend Sally Uhlmann. We ordered two different country hams, one from Kentucky and one from Virginia. Homemade biscuits were on the menu, along with a huge platter of Hoppin' John and coleslaw, both considered essential to good luck in the coming year. You don't have to order country hams, but some kind of prebaked ham with our mustard compote, Hoppin' John, biscuits, and coleslaw are a tasty, fun way to bring in the New Year.

§ Country or prebaked ham

§ Mustard Fruit Compote

§ Hoppin' John

§ Cort's Coleslaw

§ Homemade biscuits

§ Tiramisù Trifle (page 178)

Wine Tip: Sparkling wine and Chianti Classico. We love sparkling wine with rich meats, and no meat is richer to us than ham. We were trying to remember what red wine we've liked with ham and thought of prosciutto and Chianti Classico, a good combination if there ever was one, so we're sure Chianti Classico will hang in there with an American version of ham.

Mustard Fruit Compote

Serve with ham, turkey, or a prime rib of beef or pork.

1 tablespoon mustard seeds

1 teaspoon turmeric

1 teaspoon dried mustard

2 cups apple juice

15 to 20 pitted prunes, chopped

15 to 20 dried apricots, chopped

1 cup raisins

1 cup dried cranberries or cherries

6 to 8 dried figs, chopped

3 fresh pears, cored and chopped

¼ cup brown sugar

¼ cup honey mustard

1. In a small sauté pan, heat the mustard seeds and turmeric over medium heat until the seeds begin to pop, about 2 minutes. Be careful not to inhale directly over the pan, as the mustard gas is strong.

2. Put the toasted spices in a large, heavy saucepan along with the rest of the ingredients, stirring to combine. Bring to a simmer and cook until the pears are soft, about 25 minutes.

Hoppin' John

Two kinds of sausage—fresh Italian and smoked Polish—bring a different complexity to this traditional dish, which combines the cooking traditions of Africa with those of South Carolina.

1. Put the dried beans in a large pot and add water to cover by 3 to 4 inches. Soak for at least 2 hours.

2. Add the ham hocks, cinnamon stick, bay leaves, ginger, and jalapeño to the dried beans. Bring to a boil, then reduce heat and simmer.

3. Cook until the beans are tender, 1 to 2½ hours. Start checking the tenderness of the beans at about 45 minutes. When the beans are al dente, prick the Polish sausages with a fork and throw them in the pot. Add water as needed to cover.

4. Meanwhile, preheat the oven to 400°F. Prick the Italian sausages with a fork and roast them on a baking sheet for 20 minutes.

5. When the beans are tender, remove them from the heat and discard the aromatics (bay leaves, ginger, and jalapeño). Transfer the ham hocks and Polish sausage to a chopping board. Remove the meat from the hocks and chop it. Cut the Polish and Italian sausages into bite-sized pieces.

6. In a medium sauté pan, heat the oil over medium-high heat. Sauté the diced onion until it is soft.

7. Add the following to the pot of beans: the chicken stock, rice, sautéed onion, coriander, white pepper, and cayenne, the meats, and the frozen greens.

8. Bring the mixture to a simmer and cook uncovered until the rice is tender, 30 to 40 minutes. Stir every 5 minutes or so. Salt to taste.

Note: The Hoppin' John has a medium heat. If you like less heat, try any combination of the following: omit the jalapeño or cayenne, or replace the spicy Italian sausage with sweet.

1 pound dried black-eyed peas

2 ham hocks

1 stick cinnamon

2 bay leaves

2-inch piece of ginger, unpeeled

1 fresh jalapeño pepper (see Note)

1 pound each of Polish sausages and spicy Italian sausages

1 tablespoon olive oil

2 medium onions, peeled and diced

2 cups chicken stock

1½ cups long-grain white rice, Carolina brand if you can find it, but any good long-grain rice will do

½ teaspoon each of ground coriander, ground white pepper, and cayenne

1 package (1 pound) frozen collard or mustard greens

Kosher salt to taste

Cort's Coleslaw

Many years ago, Julia Child developed a recipe for coleslaw that included cumin. Our copy of the recipe disappeared a long time ago, but adding cumin to coleslaw has remained simply because it's so distinctively good. This coleslaw pairs particularly well with Hoppin' John.

¼ cup finely chopped fresh parsley

1 tart green apple, such as Granny Smith, peeled and grated

1 bunch green onions, both green and white parts, chopped

2 green bell peppers, seeded, quartered, and diced

6 cups finely sliced green cabbage (about 1 medium cabbage)

FOR THE DRESSING

1 teaspoon each of ground cumin and kosher salt

1 tablespoon Dijon mustard

Juice of ½ lemon

3 tablespoons white vinegar

⅓ cup each of sour cream and plain yogurt

½ cup mayonnaise

1. In a large bowl, combine the dressing ingredients (low-fat substitutes for the sour cream, yogurt, and mayonnaise work fine) and mix well. Stir in the parsley, grated apple, green onions, and bell peppers. Add the shredded cabbage and mix thoroughly.

2. Chill for at least 1 hour before serving. This coleslaw will keep for 2 days in the refrigerator.

Twice-Cooked Peking Lamb Shoulder

Lulu once cooked with Alice Waters for a weekend in Salina, Kansas, where Alice was on the board of the innovative Land Institute. A whole lamb had come from a local farm, and Alice and her staff from Berkeley used the shoulders for Sunday supper. Lulu remembers that the shoulders cooked for a long time in the oven, and then were put on the grill. So we tinkered with this concept and finally got the idea to serve lamb à la Peking duck. Every time we serve it, it disappears in less than 30 minutes. One lamb shoulder will do for eight people if it's going to be served with other things; two to three roasts are needed if it's the main Big Platter item. Remember, the front legs of a lamb are called the shoulders. You want the blade cut, bone in, not the boneless arm roast.

1. Preheat the oven to 375°F. Season the lamb shoulder with salt and pepper. In a deep, large skillet or sauté pan, heat the canola oil over medium-high heat and brown the shoulder for 5 to 8 minutes per side.

2. Transfer the lamb to a roasting pan, add the garlic and rosemary and 3 cups of the wine or other braising liquid. One time we used two large cans of Guinness, another time we used a bottle of Australian Shiraz.

3. Cover and roast the shoulder for 3 hours, checking midway through cooking time to see if more braising liquid should be added. The roast is done when the meat pulls away easily from the bone.

4. Prepare a hot fire in a charcoal grill. Transfer the lamb to the grill over indirect heat (coals on one side, lamb on the other) and grill for about 30 minutes, turning once. The idea is to render the last of the fat from the shoulder and crisp the skin of the meat, making the meat irresistibly crunchy while retaining its juices.

5. Let the meat rest under loosely tented foil for 15 minutes and then pull it apart with your hands, removing the meat from the bones and arranging it on a platter.

6. Heat the tortillas quickly in a dry sauté pan or over an open gas flame on your stovetop. Cut them in half. Put small bowls of all the extra stuff around the lamb platter so people can fill their own tortillas as they wish.

Wine Tip: We like the Syrah grape with lamb, either a Shiraz from Australia or a central coast California version like the wonderful Qupe Syrah.

1 lamb shoulder blade roast (3 to 4 pounds)

Kosher salt and coarsely ground pepper to taste

Canola oil, for browning the meat

1 head garlic, split in half

4 sprigs rosemary

3 to 4 cups dry red or white wine, beer, or beef stock

THE OTHER STUFF

Large flour tortillas

Chopped mint leaves

Green onions, thinly sliced

Hoisin sauce (available in Asian grocery stores)

Pickled ginger

Bean sprouts or other sprouts

Chopped romaine or iceberg lettuce or cabbage

1 cucumber, seeded and diced

Salmon with Green Curry

We remember being mesmerized the first time we ate at Terra, in St. Helena, where we had the salmon with red curry sauce. We've been experimenting with the tastes of that dish ever since. We used to make sea bass with red curry sauce until sea bass became overfished, so we went back to salmon and found we really loved the green, rather than the red, curry with it. Visually it is stunning, and it is very easy to prepare.

FOR THE SALMON

1 side (fillet) of salmon (about 4 pounds), skin on

Olive oil and coarse or kosher salt, for drizzling

1 pound snow peas, blanched

¼ cup cilantro leaves

2 tablespoons chopped fresh basil leaves

1½ tablespoons black sesame seeds

FOR THE CURRY SAUCE

3 cups each of coconut milk and chicken stock

⅓ cup Thai green curry paste

1 banana, peeled and broken into chunks

1 tart green apple, such as Granny Smith, seeded and quartered

2 stalks of lemon grass (about 6 inches each), smashed with the flat side of a chef's knife or cleaver

4 kaffir lime leaves

3-inch piece of ginger, peeled

1 tablespoon black sesame seeds

1. Combine all the ingredients for the curry sauce in a heavy saucepan. Bring to a simmer over medium-low heat and reduce to about half, stirring every once in a while. This will take a couple of hours.

2. Transfer the sauce to another saucepan and strain it back into the warm pan, as you do this pushing the banana and apple pulp through the strainer. Stir and set aside.

3. Preheat the oven to 450°F. Arrange the salmon on a baking sheet with a lip, drizzle with olive oil and sprinkle with salt, and roast for 12 minutes. The salmon is done when the thickest portion is opaque at the center. Check by turning a fork gently in the salmon.

4. With a helper and two spatulas, transfer the salmon to a platter. Return the curry sauce to the heat to rewarm it. Pour the sauce over the salmon, then add the blanched snow peas, cilantro and basil leaves, and sesame seeds. Serve with steamed jasmine rice.

Wine Tip: Pinot Noir is always good with salmon, but with all the spice going on in this dish, we think German Riesling is the ticket, a Spaetlese preferably.

Thai **Cold Beef Salad**

When cold roast beef sandwiches just won't do, try this salad. It's a great use of leftover roast beef or steaks, especially if they've been cooked to rare or medium-rare. If you don't have any leftover beef, a grilled flank steak, sliced thin, works wonderfully. The inspiration for this salad came from Thailand, where they like their salads spicy, but the heat in the dressing can be decreased or eliminated altogether by using less cayenne, or none. Note: This dish can be served on a big platter, or the ingredients can be presented separately, as shown at left, to let each diner compose their own Thai beef salad wrap, substituting leaf lettuce for iceberg.

1. Bring a large pot of water to a boil over high heat. Place the bean sprouts in a sieve or colander. Lower the sprouts into the boiling water for about 1 minute. Immediately remove and rinse under cold water until the sprouts have completely cooled. Arrange the sprouts on several layers of paper towels to drain.

2. On a big platter, arrange the shredded lettuce in an even layer. Toss in the mung bean sprouts. Loosely mound the sliced beef in the center of the greens. Sprinkle the fresh mint, green onions, cilantro, and peanuts over the salad.

3. Combine all the ingredients for the dressing in a jar with a lid. Put the lid on the jar and shake vigorously. Pour the dressing over the salad and serve cold or at room temperature.

Note: In some areas you'll be able to find bottled ginger juice—an excellent product and a real time-saver. If it's not available, simply grate a 1-inch piece of ginger with the skin on, mound it in your hand, and then squeeze it tightly right over the jar. The juice will come running.

Wine Tip: Rosé from the Bandol region of France or some California Rosé in that style. Or do as they do in Thailand and serve the salad with cold beer.

1½ cups fresh mung bean sprouts

1 head iceberg lettuce, cut into shreds

1½ to 2 pounds cooked beef, thinly sliced

¼ cup finely chopped fresh mint

1 bunch green onions, both white and green parts, chopped

¼ cup finely chopped fresh cilantro

¼ cup chopped roasted salted peanuts

FOR THE DRESSING

2 tablespoons rice wine vinegar

2 teaspoons soy sauce

½ teaspoon ginger juice (see Note)

½ teaspoon sesame oil

2 teaspoons Thai sweet chili sauce

½ teaspoon cayenne

Juice of 1 lime

Seafood Choucroute Garni

Lulu had a seafood version of choucroute garni in Paris once, in one of those Alsatian brasseries that specialize in the classic dish. She never forgot it, so we've done our best to recreate it here. It is not as carefree to put together as the smoked meat version that follows but the resulting presentation is well worth the trouble.

---

2 to 3 pounds mixed seafood, including firm white fish such as halibut and scallops, lobster tail, and shrimp

4 pounds sauerkraut, rinsed and drained

2 dozen small new potatoes

1 tablespoon juniper berries

1 teaspoon each of dried dill, mustard seeds, and caraway seeds

2 bottles (750 ml) Alsatian wine, the same you want to drink with the meal

1 quart half-and-half

1 cup chopped chives

2 to 3 dozen mussels

Selection of vegetables and herbs to cook with mussels, such as 1 or 2 stalks celery, ¼ onion, and a handful of parsley or fennel fronds

Olive oil, for baking sheet

Coarse sea salt or kosher salt, for the salmon

1 side (fillet) of salmon (2½ to 3 pounds), skin on

1. Smoke your mixed seafood per Cort's instructions on page 83. You can do this the morning of the party or the day before if it fits your schedule better. Just store and chill your smoked items, then bring them to room temperature while you assemble the rest of the dish.

2. Preheat the oven to 350°F. Assemble the sauerkraut, potatoes, and all the seasonings in a baking dish. Add two-thirds of one of your bottles of wine and toss to distribute seasonings. Cover and bake for an hour, or until the potatoes are tender.

3. At the same time you put the kraut mixture in the oven, combine a bottle of the wine and the half-and-half in a large saucepan. Simmer over medium-low heat until the mixture is reduced by half, about an hour. Add the chives and remove from the heat.

4. Clean the mussels and remove their beards. Combine the remaining one-third bottle of wine and enough additional water so you have 3 inches of liquid in a Dutch oven or stockpot. (Do not add the mussels to the pot yet.) Throw in the vegetables and herbs. When you have about 15 minutes of cooking time left for your potatoes and sauerkraut, place the mussels on top of your vegetables and liquids, cover, and steam until they open, about 15 minutes.

5. Remove the kraut mixture from the oven. Add the smoked fish and seafood to the baking dish to warm them up a bit and cover the baking dish again and set it aside. Increase the oven temperature to 450°F.

6. On a baking sheet with a lip, drizzle some good olive oil and sprinkle some coarse sea salt or kosher salt. Place the salmon on the baking sheet and roast it for 12 minutes. Check for doneness at the thickest part of the fish by inserting a fork and turning it slightly. The center should be opaque and flaky.

7. Now, to assemble: On your biggest platter, place the sauerkraut, smoked fish and seafood, and potatoes. Carefully, with someone helping you and two spatulas, slide the salmon on top of the kraut.

Place the mussels around the outside edges of the platter. Pour the sauce over the salmon and mussels. (You may want to warm the sauce to a simmer again before pouring.)

8. Take a photo—it will be that great looking.

Wine Tip: Alsatian Tokay, Pinot Gris, Sylvaner, or Riesling are made for this dish, but this is also a place to try the only red grown in Alsace, Pinot Noir. Parisian brasseries serve it slightly chilled. Use one of the white varietals in the sauerkraut and the sauce, though.

Choucroute Garni

An Alsatian specialty consisting of a variety of smoked meats, sausages, and sauerkraut, this is one of our favorite party dishes for the depths of winter. It is easy to do for a large crowd and, since all the meat is already smoked, all you are really doing is combining, spicing, and heating. If there's a smokehouse in your area, buy your pork and sausages there.

1. Preheat the oven to 375°F. Combine the sauerkraut, all the meats, the spices, and the wine in a large roasting pan.

2. Cover and bake for at least an hour. The idea is for the flavors of the meats and meat fats to permeate the sauerkraut and vice versa.

3. Cut the sausages into thirds. Remove the meat from the ham hocks.

4. The sauerkraut goes on a big platter with the pork chops around the outside, sausages and hock meat arranged on top. Serve the potatoes, mustard, and horseradish on the side.

Wine Tip: This dish is traditionally paired with the wines of its origin, Alsace, and generally this means Riesling. We happen to like it with Gewürztraminer because of all those crazy aromas and flavors in the wine. Very entertaining. This is a case where it really is worth the extra few dollars to drink the wine of the region the dish comes from.

2 pounds sauerkraut, about 4 ounces per person

8 smoked pork chops, 1 per person

8 assorted smoked sausages, such as bratwurst and knackwurst, 1 per person

2 ham hocks or shanks, 1 for every 4 people

1 teaspoon each of juniper berries and mustard seeds

2 teaspoons caraway seeds

1 bottle (750 ml) white wine, preferably from the Alsace region

FOR SERVING
16 to 24 boiled new potatoes, 2 to 3 per person

Coarse ground mustard

Grated horseradish

Greens with Leeks and Pears

Greens cooked in apple cider with the addition of pears have that wonderful yin-yang balance of sweet and slightly bitter. They are terrific with any rich meat dish, as they cut through the taste of fat on your palate. We serve them with the short ribs on page 67 or the oxtails on page 90, and they would also be fabulous with Chicken Alsace (page 94).

---

4 to 6 leeks, white part only

6 bunches of greens (about 4 pounds), either collard, mustard, or a combination

2 tablespoons each of butter and olive oil

1 to 2 cups apple cider or apple juice

2 pears, cored and cut into cubes, but not peeled

1 teaspoon kosher salt

Freshly ground pepper to taste

1. Cut the leeks into ³⁄₈-inch-thick rounds. Soak in a bowl full of water for about 20 minutes, changing the water twice and rinsing out the bowl to eliminate the sand and grit.

2. Trim the stems off the greens and discard any bad leaves. Soak and rinse the greens, using the same process as the leeks.

3. Place the leeks and greens in a colander and rinse one last time under cold water. Coarsely chop the greens.

4. In a large, heavy skillet over low heat, melt the butter and heat the olive oil. Sauté the leeks slowly until they are just tender, 15 to 20 minutes.

5. Add the coarsely chopped greens and increase the heat to medium. When the greens have wilted and their bulk is reduced by about half, add enough of the apple cider to just cover them and top with the pears. Cook for 40 minutes or more, until the greens and pears are tender, adding more apple cider or water as needed to keep the greens from burning. Season with the salt and pepper. Serve on a big platter with a lip, either hot or at room temperature.

Smoked **Seafood Salad**

We tried this very fancy main dish salad with a variety of ingredients—including smoked mussels and clams in the shell—until Cort discovered the winning combination of smoked halibut, scallops, and lobster removed from the shell. This method is the essence of simplicity; all you need is some briquettes, some smoking chips, an old colander, and patience.

We fussed with the dressing, each making our own: Lulu put down a bed of baby spinach, then the smoked items, and dressed the whole thing. Cort liked keeping the dressing on the side, so we will give you both dressing recipes and you can go from there. This is a wonderful main platter presentation for a lunch or for an over-the-top supper.

---

1. Ignite about 3 pounds of charcoal briquettes (or an equal amount of lump charcoal) in a covered kettle grill.

2. Tear off a 3-foot length of aluminum foil. Fold it in half. Place the smoking chips in the middle and fold the foil over to make a tight packet. Poke two or three small holes in the top of the packet.

3. Rinse the scallops and halibut in cold water and let them drain on several layers of paper towel.

4. Remove the raw lobster meat from the tail. This is best accomplished with a pair of poultry shears: Following both sides of the shell, cut the flat bottom shell completely out. Using a couple of potholders to protect your hands, crack the remaining shell by prying it in half.

5. Cut the halibut and the lobster into pieces about the same size as the scallops.

6. Spray the inside of the colander with a light layer of baking spray. Place the seafood mixture in the colander.

7. Once the charcoal is covered in a light gray ash, push the briquettes to one side of the grate. Place the foil-wrapped smoking chips directly on top of the coals, with the holes facing up.

8. Put the cooking grate in the grill. Position the colander filled with the seafood opposite the charcoal. Cover the grill, leaving both top and bottom vents completely open. The smoke will soon start pouring out the vents.

9. Every 15 to 20 minutes, gently stir the seafood in the colander, being careful not to break up the fish. The seafood is done when it is just uniformly opaque, a process that could take *(continued)*

1 pound sea scallops (the big guys)

1 pound firm white fish, such as halibut

1½- to 2-pound lobster, in the shell

Nonstick baking spray

3 pounds charcoal briquettes

Heavy-duty aluminum foil

1½ cups smoking chips, preferably alder wood (hickory or mesquite will do)

A colander that you don't mind getting smoky and permanently discolored

FOR THE SALAD
4 cups baby spinach, cleaned

1 English cucumber, sliced thin

4 oranges, peeled and sliced, seeds removed

1 bunch asparagus or 2 cups green beans, blanched

½ cup toasted hazelnuts, roughly chopped (see Note, page 18)

1 recipe Lulu's or Cort's Dressing (recipes follow)

1½ to 2 hours. Transfer the smoked seafood to a bowl. Cover with plastic wrap and reserve in the refrigerator until needed.

10. Arrange all the salad elements prettily on a large platter. Add the seafood. Dress or undress—the salad, that is.

Wine Tip: Viognier, the wonderful white varietal from the Rhône and now California, would be a breathtaking accompaniment.

Lulu's Dressing

½ **cup fresh orange juice**

¼ **cup raspberry vinegar**

Dash each of soy sauce, sesame oil, hot sauce, and kosher salt

2 **tablespoons canola oil**

½ **cup sesame seeds**

1. Combine the orange juice, vinegar, soy, sesame oil, hot sauce, and salt in a small mixing bowl.

2. In a small sauté pan, heat the oil and brown the sesame seeds over medium to low heat. Don't leave these guys alone or something black and smoky will happen. When they start to turn golden brown, remove from the heat and pour right into the acid mixture. This will prevent them from continuing to cook. Give the dressing a good stir and it's ready to pour over the seafood.

Cort's Dressing

⅓ **cup mild-flavored vegetable oil, such as canola**

Juice of 1 lemon

Juice of 1 orange

2 **teaspoons rice wine vinegar**

2 **tablespoons finely chopped fresh parsley**

¼ **teaspoon ground white pepper**

Salt to taste

Combine all the ingredients in a jar with a lid. Shake vigorously.

Valentine's Day Feast

All you single cooks out there: next Valentine's Day rally your friends for an elegant supper that will make you glad to be unattached. Or if you're coupled: invite your best paired-up pals and celebrate love together for a change. Just send everyone home early so they can exchange their Valentine gifts the old-fashioned way: couples only.

§ **Grilled Oysters (page 13)**
§ **Prosecco Risotto and Four Cheeses**
§ **Sautéed Scallop and Lobster Salad**
§ **Breadsticks or sourdough rolls**
§ **Flourless Chocolate Torte (page 176)**

Wine Tip: The Prosecco you use for the risotto is a perfect wine for the evening, light and celebratory at the same time.

Prosecco Risotto and Four Cheeses

We wanted a very stylish luxury version of risotto for the season, something celebratory you could serve on special occasions. We can report that when we make this dish, the bowl is empty in no time flat. Get your portion early.

1. In a large, heavy sauté pan, heat 2 tablespoons of the butter and the oil over low heat. Sauté the onion until it is translucent, stirring often, about 7 minutes. Add the rice and toss to coat it with the oil.

2. In a separate saucepan, heat your stock and the bottle of Prosecco. Ladle the liquid onto the rice just to cover. Let it simmer until the moisture has been absorbed, then ladle more on, stirring often during this process. The quantity is always an approximation, as the amount of liquid that can be absorbed will vary according to the water content of the rice, the humidity, and more.

3. If you are going to stop cooking for the day, do it when the rice is still crunchy in the middle. See page 41 for more information.

4. When you have used about half the liquid, add all the cheeses but the Parmesan. Continue adding liquid and stirring until the rice kernels are just tender in the middle, usually about 40 minutes total. Stir in the last tablespoon of butter and the Parmesan.

5. Turn the risotto out on a platter with a lip and garnish with parsley.

2 tablespoons butter, plus 1 tablespoon more to finish the dish

2 tablespoons olive oil

1 medium onion, peeled and diced small

2 cups Arborio rice

2½ quarts liquid including 1 bottle (750 ml) Prosecco sparkling wine plus chicken or vegetable stock

4 ounces each of Gruyère, Gorgonzola, mascarpone, and grated Parmesan cheese

Italian (flat-leaf) parsley leaves

Sautéed Scallop and Lobster Salad

How can you fail to impress with so many quality ingredients? Not only will this main course salad make your Valentine feel loved, it's a great way to wow guests for a special birthday lunch or a wedding brunch.

---

2 pounds bay or sea scallops

1 large lobster tail, removed from the shell and sliced into ¼-inch slices

3 grapefruit, peeled and sectioned

2 cups sugar snap peas, blanched, rinsed, rolled in a paper towel to dry, and chilled in the refrigerator

1 bunch asparagus, tips only, treated like the sugar snaps

1 mango, peeled and diced

½ cup roughly chopped roasted salted peanuts

2 fresh jalapeño peppers, sliced thin

½ cup each of chopped basil leaves and whole cilantro leaves, for garnish

FOR THE MARINADE

½ cup each of good sherry (dry or semidry), rice wine vinegar, and Thai sweet chili sauce

¼ cup each of sesame oil and canola oil

Juice of 1 grapefruit

1. Combine all the marinade ingredients, divide between two bowls, and add the scallops to one bowl and the lobster to the other. Cover and chill for 2 hours but not much more than that or the acid will "cook" the scallops.

2. Heat a large, dry sauté pan and start cooking the seafood in batches. Sauté the scallops and the lobster slices separately. Stand right there and give each batch a minute or two a side, turning carefully with tongs or a slotted spoon. Try not to tear the seafood up. Since they're the largest, the sea scallops will take the longest, 5 minutes total, but they don't have to be cooked clear through, as they will continue to cook off the heat.

3. As you finish one batch, remove it with a slotted spoon onto your serving platter. In between batches, let the pan reheat for a minute before you put in more seafood. The coating of marinade on the seafood should be plenty of moisture to sauté in.

4. When you are done cooking the seafood, pour the remaining marinade in the sauté pan and simmer it for 5 minutes. This is your dressing. Let it cool in the pan until needed. Although preparing the seafood sounds tedious, it won't take more than 20 minutes or so, and you can do it all before your guests arrive.

5. Now you have a mound of delicious seafood on your platter. Start adding your other ingredients, from the grapefruit sections to the jalapeño slices. You can compose or you can throw them in. We're "throwers," but this lineup of ingredients is so colorful, you can't go wrong. Now dress the salad. Top it with the basil and cilantro garnish. You can put this salad right on the serving table, but if you do, you have to cover it or it will be picked at and eaten before you say "Come and get it." Hide it in the refrigerator if you have room.

Pork Chops Smothered in Onions and Apples

This is a hearty winter meal, sure to please just about everyone. The pork chops remain succulent and are nicely complemented by the sweet apples and tart onions. Easy and quick to prepare, this dish is great with a big platter of buttered, parslied egg noodles.

---

2 tablespoons each of butter and vegetable oil

2 medium onions, sliced in half from top to bottom, then cut into thin, half round slices

3 large green apples, such as Granny Smith, peeled, cored, and cut into ⅜-inch-thick slices

1 can (14 ounces) regular-strength chicken stock

8 center-cut pork loin chops (bone-in or boneless), about 1 inch thick

Kosher salt and ground white pepper to taste

1 tablespoon balsamic vinegar

½ cup sour cream

1 teaspoon paprika

1 bunch chives, finely chopped

1. Melt 1 tablespoon of the butter and 1 tablespoon of the oil in a large skillet over medium-high heat. Reduce the heat to medium, add the onions and apples, and sauté until the onions are wilted, stirring constantly, 8 to 10 minutes. Add the stock and bring just to a boil. Remove from the heat and set aside.

2. Season the pork chops with salt and white pepper. In another large skillet (one that can accommodate all of the chops), melt the remaining 1 tablespoon butter and 1 tablespoon oil over high heat. Add the chops and brown them quickly, 1 minute per side. As soon as they have been browned, sprinkle them with the balsamic vinegar, shaking the pan as you do.

3. Immediately reduce the heat to low, top the chops with the onion and apple mixture, along with the stock, and cover the pan. Cook for approximately 8 minutes for boneless chops, or 10 minutes for bone-in chops. The chops are done when there's just a hint of pink at the center when cut.

4. Transfer the chops to a large, heated platter. Remove the pan from the heat and add the sour cream to the apple and onion mixture. Stir until the sauce is smooth and pour it over the chops on the platter. Dust with paprika and sprinkle with chopped chives.

Wine Tip: This is one time when a dish can stand up to a big, toasty, fruity California Chardonnay.

Oxtails with Green Olives

Serve this dish and you'll be amazed at how many closeted oxtail-lovers there are, most of whom will exclaim, "I haven't had this since I was a kid!" A delicacy worth reviving if there ever was one. You could make it all in one day, but please don't. Cook the oxtails for a couple of hours the day before you need them and finish them off the day of serving. It makes such a difference in flavor.

4 to 5 pounds oxtails

2 teaspoons kosher salt

1 teaspoon black pepper

2 tablespoons each of canola oil, olive oil, and butter

1 large or 2 medium onions, peeled and sliced

2 carrots, peeled and sliced

4 stalks celery, sliced

4 to 6 cloves garlic, peeled and sliced

1 bottle (750 ml) Rhône wine (a Côtes du Rhône will work fine)

4 cups veal or chicken stock

4 leeks, sliced up into the green about ½ inch, soaked and rinsed

½ pound green olives, oil-cured and pitted

2 fennel bulbs, tops and bottoms removed, sliced

1. Season the oxtails with the salt and pepper. In a heavy Dutch oven or large, heavy pot with a tightly fitting lid, brown the oxtails in the canola and olive oils over medium heat, 10 to 12 minutes. Remove them and set aside.

2. Melt the butter in the same pot and add the rough mirepoix (onions, carrots, and celery) and the garlic. Sauté slowly over medium-low heat until the onions wilt, about 10 minutes.

3. Add the oxtails to the mirepoix with the bottle of wine and 2 cups of the stock. Simmer, covered, for 2 hours, stirring every once in a while. This is the place to stop, store, and start again tomorrow.

4. If you did stop and store, return the sauce (but not the oxtails) to the Dutch oven and reheat it slowly, adding the remaining 2 cups stock. If you are cooking this all in one day, just continue. Add the leeks, olives, and fennel to the sauce, then reintroduce the oxtails to the pot. Cover and simmer for 2 hours over low heat, stirring occasionally. The oxtails are done when the meat is very tender and pulls away easily from the bone.

5. In a fancy restaurant, you would remove the meat from the bones, but we don't have to do that. Just turn this out on a big platter, and serve it with some mashed potatoes, Lulu's Root Bake (page 29), or rice. The fun is in finding those wonderful morsels of meat that have basted in their own juices.

Wine Tip: These difficult-to-match food items like olives and fennel call out for wines from the South of France. Try something from the much improved Languedoc-Roussillon regions.

Joe's Special

Sometime long ago in the seventies, a restaurant opened in Kansas City with a San Francisco theme. That was the first time Lulu tasted Joe's eggs, a famous San Francisco dish of eggs scrambled with ground beef and spinach. Cort grew up in the San Francisco Bay Area and ate Joe's Special all his life. We know you can't make scrambled eggs to order for a group, so we figured out a way to make Joe's Special in a baked style. The classic version includes hot sauce; we added a little extra heat with the jalapeño. The potatoes and cheese are additions that we like. We've also heard of mushrooms being added, to glowing reviews, and of the ground beef replaced with drained cooked Italian sausage, the hot version. Sounds good to us.

---

1. Preheat the oven to 375°F. Brown the ground beef and onion in a sauté pan and then put it in a large round casserole that has been sprayed with nonstick baking spray.

2. In the same sauté pan, over medium heat, wilt the spinach. This will take about 5 minutes. Distribute the spinach evenly over the ground beef. You could just put the fresh spinach in the casserole—it would certainly cook—but we think wilting it first reduces the amount of moisture that will release into the eggs. If you are in a hurry and have to throw the spinach in raw, reduce the water you add to the eggs by half.

3. Put half of the cheese, both Monterey Jack and Parmesan, over the spinach. Place the potatoes on top of the cheese layer.

4. Combine the eggs, water, sour cream, hot sauce, and jalapeño, and season with salt and pepper. Pour the egg mixture over the layers and cover with the rest of the cheese.

5. Bake until the eggs are set and the top is brown. The time this takes will depend on the depth of your dish, but it will probably be between 35 to 50 minutes. Remove from the oven and let set 2 or 3 minutes. Invert the eggs onto a serving platter.

6. If you don't want to bother with the inversion procedure, it won't hurt a thing. Just let the scrambled eggs cool for 10 minutes before you cut the casserole in wedges and serve it out of the baking dish.

1 pound ground beef

1 onion, peeled and diced

Nonstick baking spray, for the casserole dish

1 pound fresh spinach (about 1 bunch)

1/2 pound Monterey Jack cheese, grated

2 tablespoons grated Parmesan cheese

1 pound new potatoes, cooked and diced

12 eggs, lightly beaten

1/2 cup each of water and sour cream

1 teaspoon hot sauce

1 fresh jalapeño pepper, seeded and sliced

Kosher salt and pepper to taste

North Beach Veal Stew

This is an Italian version of the famous French stew *blanquette de veau.* In both versions the veal is not browned, but there the similarities end. This fragrant recipe, reminiscent of Italian stews served in San Francisco's North Beach in the 1950s, features artichoke hearts, olives, and tomatoes. It is excellent served with egg noodles tossed with butter and chopped parsley.

1 cup dry vermouth

2 cups dry white wine

2 cups shallots, peeled and sliced (substitute onions if necessary)

2 bay leaves

3-inch sprig of fresh rosemary, or 1½ teaspoons dried rosemary

4 to 5 cloves garlic, peeled and finely chopped

1 teaspoon kosher salt

½ teaspoon freshly ground pepper

4 pounds veal stew meat

1 pound mushrooms, quartered

2 cans (13 ounces each) artichoke hearts (packed in water), drained and cut in half

1 can (28 ounces) diced tomatoes, including the juice

¾ cup oil-cured, pitted olives, such as calamata

Chopped fresh parsley, for garnish

1. Preheat the oven to 350°F. Place the vermouth, wine, shallots, bay leaves, rosemary, garlic, salt, and pepper in a large ovenproof saucepan. Bring to a boil and add the veal stew meat. Cook until the veal turns white, 5 to 7 minutes. Cover and cook in the oven, for 45 minutes.

2. Remove from the oven and add the mushrooms, artichoke hearts, tomatoes, and olives. Return to the oven and cook, uncovered, for an additional 60 minutes, or until the veal is tender. Top with chopped parsley and serve it forth.

Wine Tip: Barbera d'Alba or Barbera d'Asti. Barbera is such a good wine to pair with tomato-based dishes since the acidity of this wine matches the acidity of tomatoes. Michele Chiarlo is a great producer of the d'Asti version, as well as other great Piedmont wines.

Chicken Alsace

The classic French chicken dishes such as coq au vin are ideal for Big Platter cooking, but you don't need us to tell you how to make coq au vin. However, we spotted a coq au Riesling that captured our attention in Anne Willan's classic *French Regional Cooking* (now, sadly, out-of-print). For a new twist on this French big platter classic, we changed the Riesling to a spicy Gewürztraminer, and added some apples and some crispy shallots on the top.

---

2 whole chickens (6 to 7 pounds total), cut up

1 cup flour

1 teaspoon each of kosher salt, ground white pepper, and paprika

3 tablespoons vegetable oil, plus additional oil for frying the shallots

3 tablespoons butter

8 shallots, peeled and sliced

1 bottle (750 ml) Gewürztraminer

3 or 4 sprigs fresh thyme

2 bay leaves

4 sprigs parsley

¼ teaspoon ground nutmeg

¼ cup cognac

1 pound mushrooms, sliced

Juice of 1 lemon

3 cooking apples (such as Jonathan, Granny Smith, or Braeburn), peeled and cut into ½-inch slices

1 cup (½ pint) heavy cream

1. Rinse the chicken pieces in cold water and pat them dry with paper towels. Combine the flour, salt, white pepper, and paprika. Dust the chicken pieces on all sides with the flour mixture.

2. In a large, heavy skillet, melt 2 tablespoons of the oil and 2 tablespoons of the butter over medium-high heat. Add the chicken pieces to the skillet without crowding them; brown on both sides, 8 to 10 minutes total. Reserve browned chicken on a platter until needed.

3. Reduce the heat to medium and sauté three of the shallots until just tender. Place the chicken in a large pan (with a cover) and add the sautéed shallots. Pour the Gewürztraminer over the chicken and shallots. Add the thyme, bay leaves, parsley, and nutmeg.

4. Add the cognac to the skillet the chicken was sautéed in. Carefully ignite it with a match (turn off the exhaust fan) and swirl it gently around the skillet. Pour it into the pan with the chicken. Cover the pan and cook over medium-low heat for 30 minutes.

5. Meanwhile, using a paper towel, wipe out the skillet. Place it over medium heat and melt the remaining 1 tablespoon oil and 1 tablespoon butter. Add the mushrooms, sprinkle with the lemon juice, and sauté until just tender, 12 to 15 minutes.

6. After the chicken has cooked for 30 minutes, remove the cover and add the sautéed mushrooms, sliced apples, and cream. Replace the cover and cook for an additional 30 minutes.

7. Heat about ½ inch of vegetable oil in a medium sauté pan. When the oil is hot but not smoking, reduce the heat to low and add the remaining shallots, turning often with a slotted spoon or tongs. When the shallots are browned and crisp, take them out of the oil, and drain on a paper towel. Serve the chicken with shallots on top.

Wine Tip: Alsatian Gewürztraminer should be used in and drunk with the dish. The spiciness is great with the apples and the shallots.

Lamb Shanks in Guinness

This is a recipe our friend and chef Amy Newman brought to Cafe Lulu. People still ask for the recipe, and now we are sharing it with you because it is so good and easy to prepare. Make mashed potatoes, drizzle them with truffle oil if you're feeling rich, mound them in the middle of a big round platter, and place the shanks around the potatoes, bone up. Skim your pan sauce to remove the fat, and then pour some of the juices over the whole thing. It won't be pretty, but it sure is good.

---

1. Preheat the oven to 375°F. Dredge the lamb shanks in the flour, then salt and pepper them.

2. In a large sauté pan, heat the canola oil over medium heat. Brown the shanks on all sides, about 12 minutes total.

3. Place the rosemary and garlic, split side down, in a large, deep roasting pan. Put the shanks on top of the garlic and rosemary. Add the stout and apricot nectar. Braise in the oven, covered, for 2 hours.

4. Remove from the oven, skim off the fat, and baste the lamb with the pan sauce. Turn the shanks and bake them uncovered for another hour. When done, the shanks should be browned, with a caramelized surface.

5. Remove the meat, garlic skins, and rosemary from the roasting pan. Skim off the fat again. Mash the garlic pulp into the pan sauce. Arrange the shanks on a platter, pour the pan sauce over them, and serve.

Wine Tip: Lamb is often paired with big Cabernet Sauvignon, whether from California or Bordeaux. And we know that's a match. Lulu is not much of a Cab person so we're going for Zinfandel with this dish. There are many delicious Zins made in California. Ridge and Ravenswood are the old favorites that made it famous around the world. Rosenblum and St. Francis old vines are some of our new favorites.

8 large lamb shanks, or 1 per person

¾ cup flour

Kosher salt and freshly ground pepper to taste

⅓ cup canola oil

1 head garlic, split crosswise

6 sprigs rosemary

3 cans (12 ounces each) Guinness stout

3 cans (11.5 ounces each) apricot nectar

Hosting a Mardi Gras party is just about the most fun you can have and one of the best gifts you can give to your friends in the winter. Be sure to buy some Mardi Gras beads and a Louis Armstrong CD. Make a big platter of jambalaya, some muffaletas, and real New Orleans–style barbecue shrimp, and let the good times roll.

§ **Muffaletas**
§ **Lulu's Jambalaya**
§ **New Orleans Barbecue Shrimp**
§ **Bread Pudding with Pears and Pine Nuts (page 184)**

Wine Tip: We all know Cajun food loves beer, and so serve a variety of boutique beers. But we love wine, so think about how Chardonnay would work with the shrimp and crab in the jambalaya. If the barbecue shrimp are the star of the table, ask your wine merchant for a German Riesling with just a little sweetness.

How to Build a Muffaleta

Muffaleta is truly a New Orleans sandwich. The special round bread that is made for them, the olive salad that drips oil on your hands—all this is impossible to recreate. But we've made a good muffaleta imitation that can be a part of your Mardi Gras celebration, unless you live in New Orleans where you don't need this. You can go get the real thing. The addition of cream cheese in this recipe is ours and not a New Orleans' thing. We've found that it keeps the olives in the sandwich, and not all over the floor.

1. Choose a loaf of French or Italian bread that has a crisp crust. Split the bread in half lengthwise, scoop out an indentation in the rounded half, and discard the scooped out bread so the sandwich won't be too thick to handle. Drizzle this half with olive oil.

2. Line the oiled side of the bread with slices of prepared Italian meats such as salami, pepperoni, mortadella, capocollo—any combination you like. Top with a layer of Provolone cheese.

3. In a mixing bowl, mix 8 ounces softened cream cheese with 1 cup pimento-stuffed salad olives, ½ cup chopped pickled pepperoncini, and lots of freshly ground black pepper. Spread the flat side of the bread with this mixture and put it on top of the Provolone. You can also add roasted red peppers, grilled eggplant slices, or grilled onions to the sandwich fillings.

4. Wrap the sandwich tightly in plastic wrap and refrigerate for at least an hour. Each loaf can be cut into 12 to 15 strips for serving.

Lulu's Jambalaya

Figuring out a different take on a dish as well known as jambalaya was a challenge: the addition of artichoke hearts and colored peppers would probably get us drummed out of Paul Prudhomme's kitchen, but they work nicely because of the color and texture they add. The roasted garlic contributes sweetness and the shrimp stock, complexity. If you don't have time to make the shrimp stock (or you get a good deal on already peeled shrimp), simply substitute an equal amount of chicken stock.

1. In a large, heavy Dutch oven or soup pot, heat the oil over medium heat. Add the New Orleans "trinity"—onion, celery, and bell peppers—which substitutes for the French mirepoix of onions, celery, and carrots. When the vegetables have softened and the onion is translucent, 7 to 10 minutes, add the rice and toss to coat.

2. Add the chicken stock, oregano, thyme, canned tomatoes, and tomato sauce. Squeeze the roasted garlic pulp into the pot. Simmer for 20 minutes, then add the cherry tomatoes, artichoke hearts, and the sausages.

3. When the pot is running out of liquid, after about 20 more minutes, add the shrimp stock, hot sauces, Worcestershire, cayenne, and salt and pepper to taste. Taste every once in a while to test the rice. When the rice is just tender, after a total of about 40 minutes, throw in the shrimp and crabmeat. Simmer just long enough for the shrimp to turn pink, about 6 minutes, then remove from the heat.

4. Adjust seasonings and serve in a large bowl or platter with a lip. Jambalaya should be enjoyed hot. If you can't do spicy, omit the two hot sauces.

To roast the garlic

Drizzle 1 tablespoon good olive oil and a sprinkling of kosher salt into a baking pan. Split the head of garlic and place it in the pan face down. Bake in a 350°F oven for 20 minutes or so, until the garlic is soft and browned on the bottom.

To make the shrimp stock

Peel the shrimp and place the shells in a large saucepan. Add the tops and bottom of one bunch celery, some parsley stems, half an onion with the skin on, and a carrot that has been washed but not peeled. If there is an open bottle of white wine in the refrigerator, throw that in. Cover the shells with 2 quarts of cold water and bring to a boil. Reduce the heat and simmer, skimming the *(continued)*

¼ cup olive oil

1 large onion, peeled and diced

3 stalks celery, sliced thin

1 green and 1 red or yellow bell pepper, seeded, quartered, and diced

1 pound long-grain white rice

1 quart chicken stock

¼ cup chopped fresh oregano leaves

2 sprigs thyme

1 large can (28 ounces) diced tomatoes

1 small can (13 ounces) tomato sauce

1 whole head roasted garlic (see directions)

12 to 15 cherry tomatoes, halved

1 can (13 ounces) artichoke hearts, drained and quartered

1 pound Polish sausages or andouille

1 quart shrimp stock (see directions for homemade)

1 tablespoon each of Louisiana hot sauce, green Tabasco or other hot sauce, and Worcestershire sauce

1 teaspoon cayenne

Kosher salt, black pepper, and ground white pepper to taste

1 pound large uncooked shrimp (20 count), shelled and deveined

1 pound lump crabmeat

top of the stock occasionally, until you have reduced your liquid by half, about 30 minutes. Strain and cool.

Variations: If you are going to serve the New Orleans Barbecue Shrimp as well as Lulu's Jambalaya, you can substitute a pound of boneless, skinless chicken breasts for the shrimp in this dish. Cut the breasts in half, then in narrow strips, and put these in when you add the rice. Or you could have it all: chicken, sausage, crab, and shrimp!

New Orleans Barbecue Shrimp

New Orleaneans have their own way of doing things. Barbecue shrimp has nothing to do with slow cooking over a wood or charcoal fire. But the tradition of eating these messy, delicious crustaceans is one worth starting at your house if you're not already a fan. Serve with lots of French bread to sop up the sauce.

4 pounds large uncooked shrimp (20 count), heads on and unpeeled if possible

¼ cup chopped fresh parsley, for garnish

FOR THE BARBECUE SAUCE
½ cup (1 stick) butter

½ cup olive oil

Juice of 2 fresh lemons

3 cloves garlic, peeled and minced

½ cup Tabasco or other Louisiana hot sauce

2 tablespoons Worcestershire sauce

¼ cup Thai sweet chili sauce or sriracha chili-garlic sauce

1 teaspoon paprika, sweet or hot

⅓ cup mixed fresh herbs, your choice of thyme, tarragon, oregano, or chervil

Kosher salt and freshly ground pepper

1. Rinse the shrimp in cold water and allow them to drain in a colander. In a large saucepan, combine all the barbecue sauce ingredients and simmer for 5 minutes. Remove from the heat and allow the sauce to cool.

2. Place the shrimp in a large bowl. Pour the cooled sauce over the shrimp. Cover the bowl and marinate the shrimp in the refrigerator for 2 hours, stirring occasionally.

3. Preheat the oven to 375°F. Place the marinated shrimp in a large shallow baking dish. Bake for 20 minutes, turning the shrimp often, until the shells turn pink. Serve hot or at room temperature, in a large bowl topped with chopped parsley.

Big Platter Spring

For a cook, spring is an exciting time. The heavy dishes that are so appealing in January are replaced with lighter fare. Religious holidays call for family and friends to share our tables, and we love to cook for them. Along with tradition, the food offerings of spring give us inspiration. There are more choices, and cooking seems full of possibility again. Lamb, eggs, wild mushrooms, baby limas—these are some of the elements of spring cuisine. It's enough to make your mouth water just thinking about it.

Mixed Grill with Provençal Sauce

It all began with our friendly neighborhood "big box" warehouse, Costco. Their lamb chops are wonderful, great for grilling. We found it fun to pair them with another meat, such as duck, quail, or chicken breasts, giving this dish a modern spin on the classic "mixed grill." You could also make a double chop mixed grill of pork and lamb chops. Then there are the accompaniments: we like spaghetti squash instead of the more traditional potato or pasta. And the Provençal Sauce features the bounty of fresh produce.

1. Preheat the oven to 400°F. Split the squash in half and discard the seeds. Bake them split side down on a baking sheet until tender, about 40 minutes. Remove from the oven, turn them cut side up, and let them cool for at least 10 minutes. Run a fork through the cooked squash meat. When the bulk of the cooked squash has been loosened from the skin, put it in a bowl, add the butter and salt and pepper, and toss. Cover the bowl with foil or a plate to keep the squash warm.

2. Prepare a charcoal or gas-fired grill. Grill your choice of meat directly over a moderately hot fire. For lamb chops, turn every 4 to 5 minutes; they will be medium rare in a total cooking time of 12 to 14 minutes. Quail are much easier to grill if their backbones are removed and the quail are flattened with the palm of your hand. (Look for European-style semi-boneless quail with the backbones removed.) Turn the quail every 3 to 4 minutes and grill for a total cooking time of 10 to 12 minutes. Duck and chicken breasts should be turned every 3 to 4 minutes and will cook in 10 to 14 minutes. Turn pork chops (approximately 1 inch thick) every 3 to 4 minutes for a total cooking time of 10 to 14 minutes.

3. Pile the squash in the middle of a big platter, place one grilled meat on one side of the squash, and the other grilled meat on the opposite side. Dress both the squash and the meats with the Provençal Sauce.

2 spaghetti squash (about 8 pounds total)

3 tablespoons butter

Kosher salt and freshly ground pepper to taste

A selection of meats to grill (about 6 pounds total): lamb chops, quail, duck breasts, chicken breasts, pork chops (choose two and then plan on 1 chop and 1 quail per person, or a half chicken or duck breast per person)

1 recipe Provençal Sauce (page 102)

Provençal Sauce

1/3 cup olive oil

4 cloves garlic, peeled and sliced

1 medium fennel bulb, top removed,
  bulb thinly sliced

2 medium zucchini, sliced

1/3 cup wine, red or white depending on what
  meats you are grilling

6 Roma tomatoes or 3 home-grown
  tomatoes, diced

1 can (about 15 ounces) garbanzo beans,
  drained

2 tablespoons fresh thyme

1 cup calamata olives, or use both black
  and green olives, about 1/2 cup each

1/4 cup capers, drained

Heat the olive oil in a medium saucepan or large sauté pan over medium heat. Add the garlic, fennel, and zucchini and reduce the heat to low. Sauté for 5 minutes; add the wine, tomatoes, garbanzo beans, and thyme. Sauté until the fennel and squash are tender, about 10 minutes more. Add the olives and capers and remove from the heat. The sauce can be served warm or at room temperature.

Wine Tip: Since this sauce is filled with flavors of southern France, we'd choose a Rhône from that district: Châteauneuf-du-Pape, Côtes du Rhône, or Gigondas.

Grilled Spring Chicken Dijon

The term "spring chicken" isn't used much anymore. Essentially a baby chicken, weighing in at 1½ to 2 pounds, you may encounter them marketed as pollito or by the French term poussin. Whatever you call them, they're tender and delicious, especially when grilled. You can safely count on one bird for two people. The easiest way to grill them is cut out the rib cage and flatten them with the heel of your hand (or ask your butcher to do this for you).

1. Mix all the marinade ingredients together, including the hot red pepper, if using. Rinse the chickens, pat them dry with paper towels, and place them in a large container. Pour the marinade over them, making sure to coat all the chickens evenly. Cover and allow to marinate in the refrigerator for 2 to 4 hours.

2. Remove the chickens from the refrigerator 30 minutes prior to grilling. Heat a gas or charcoal grill.

3. Grill the chickens directly over a hot fire, turning them every 5 minutes or so. Total cooking time will be between 20 and 30 minutes, depending on your fire and the grilling conditions.

Wine Tip: Pinot Noir is one of the best wine varietals for food: you could drink it with most of our food and be just fine. But Pinot Noir is especially good with chicken, and to get better acquainted with this grape, I'd decide on a region, in this case Oregon, and buy a couple of different bottles of Pinot Noir from that state to go with your spring chickens. Adelsheim, Erath, and Patricia Green are some wineries to look for.

4 spring chickens (approximately 8 pounds total), rib cages removed and chickens flattened

FOR THE MARINADE
⅔ cup Dijon mustard

⅓ cup olive oil

1 teaspoon dried rosemary, crumbled

½ teaspoon hot red pepper flakes (optional)

½ teaspoon freshly ground pepper

½ teaspoon kosher salt

Veal Shanks in White Wine

Who doesn't love the satisfying richness of a traditional osso buco? But when the tulips bloom and the temperatures rise, you might still hunger for the robustness of this long-cooked dish but want it lighter, less wintery. This version of braised veal shanks is from the south of France instead of Italy. It's a great way to enjoy those white Rhône wines, in the cooking and also for drinking.

½ cup olive oil

8 to 12 veal shanks, one per person

Flour, for dredging

1 onion, peeled and diced

3 carrots, peeled and diced

4 stalks celery, diced

3 fennel bulbs, sliced into rounds and chopped

4 leeks, white parts only, sliced and soaked

2 teaspoons kosher salt

Freshly ground pepper to taste

1 bottle (750 ml) white Rhône wine

Additional wine, water, or chicken stock, if necessary

FOR THE GREMOLATA
Zest of 1 grapefruit

½ cup chopped parsley leaves

2 tablespoons minced garlic

1. Preheat the oven to 375°F. In a large sauté pan, heat the oil to medium heat. Clip the membrane around each shank so the meat will lay evenly as it cooks. Dredge the shanks in the flour and brown them on both sides, about 10 minutes total. Remove the browned shanks and place them in a deep roasting pan with the marrow side of the shanks up.

2. In the same sauté pan, sauté the onion, carrots, celery, fennel, and leeks until they soften up, about 15 minutes. Remove from the heat and add the vegetables to the roasting pan with the shanks. Add the salt and pepper to taste and the wine. Cover the pan and braise for 1½ hours.

3. After 2 hours, make sure you still have moisture in the pan. Add more wine, water, or chicken stock if needed. Baste the shanks carefully, cover, and braise another hour. Take off the cover and bake another 30 to 60 minutes. The shanks are done when the meat can be easily pulled from the bone.

4. Combine the gremolata ingredients in a small bowl. Turn out the contents of the roasting pan onto a big platter and garnish with the gremolata. Try to keep the shanks marrow side up so your guests can dig the marrow out of the bones and enjoy it on pieces of bread.

Wine Tips: You make a commitment right away to what you are going to drink when you cook this dish, as you should serve a compatible wine. I think it's a terrific excuse for white Rhônes from the southern Rhône region, such as a Côtes du Rhône blanc, Hermitage blanc, or St. Joseph. FYI: There is an inexpensive wine from this region that would do just fine for cooking. It's called Parallel 45. You can drink it with the veal, too, when the bank balance runs low.

Spring Lunch for Easter or Passover

One of the miracles of modern life is the availability of almost any type of produce at any time of the year. That said, we're firm believers in celebrating each season and its holidays with its unique specialties. This menu is a memorable celebration of the best spring has to offer.

§ Fresh Limas and Barley Salad
§ Potato and Celeriac Faux Dauphine
§ Grilled Butterflied Leg of Lamb
§ Flourless Chocolate Torte (page 176)

Wine Tip: Since this is a special holiday menu that centers around grilled lamb, it is a perfect place to splurge on some good bottles of Australian Shiraz. Henschke and Penfolds make superior versions. At the lower end of the pricing spectrum, there's the largest bottling of Shiraz from Rosemount. There are excellent Kosher bottlings now. Ask your wine seller.

Fresh Limas and Barley Salad

Even if you never liked the lifeless renditions of lima beans that were forced on you in your childhood, you will love the fresh version. The saltiness of the ham is just the right contrast to the creaminess of the limas. However, you can omit the ham hock and sliced ham for a meatless menu.

1. Wash and drain the beans and then put them in a large stockpot and cover with warm water. Let them soak about 25 minutes, then bring to a boil. Add the parsley stems, onion, and ham hock. Simmer until the beans are tender, 30 minutes to 1½ hours, depending on the moisture content of the beans and their freshness. When the beans are tender, drain and cool them.

2. Remove the ham hock, let it cool, then take the meat off the bone and chop it.

3. In a medium sauté pan, heat the canola oil over medium heat and fry the slice of ham until the fat has melted or turned crunchy and the ham is nicely browned. This will take about 7 minutes per side. Remove from the heat, drain the ham slice, and dice it.

4. Combine the cooked beans, the cooked barley, the chopped parsley, and the ham from both the hock and the ham slice. Season with the salt and pepper and the thyme. Toss with the oil and vinegar and mound on a large platter.

2 pounds fresh lima beans or other fresh shelled beans

1 bunch parsley, stems reserved, washed, drained, and chopped

1 onion, peeled and quartered

1 smoked ham hock

1 tablespoon canola oil

1 slice ham, about 1 inch thick

2 cups cooked barley

1½ teaspoons kosher salt

1 teaspoon freshly ground pepper

¼ cup fresh thyme leaves, if available, or ½ teaspoon dried thyme

1½ cups walnut oil

¾ cup malt vinegar

Potato and Celeriac Faux Dauphine

Pommes (that's potatoes) Dauphine is a famous French specialty that's rarely made these days, at least in America. Classically, mashed potatoes are combined with *choux* (cream-puff) pastry dough, formed into balls, rolled in breadcrumbs, and then deep-fried. They are delicious little nuggets, crunchy on the outside and fluffy on the inside. We took the basic concept and changed it a bit. First we added celeriac (also known as celery root) to the mashed potatoes because potatoes and celery are a great flavor combination. Instead of deep-frying the mixture, we simply scattered the cooking dish and the top of the mashed mixture with breadcrumbs and then cooked the whole lot in a very hot oven. Interestingly, the results were very similar to the real *pommes* Dauphine: crunchy on the outside, fluffy on the inside, not to mention delicious.

5 large brown-skinned potatoes
(about 4 pounds)

2 to 3 celeriac roots

½ cup milk

1 cup water

½ cup (1 stick) butter

½ teaspoon kosher salt

1 cup flour

4 eggs

½ cup dried breadcrumbs

Butter-flavored baking spray

1. Preheat the oven to 400°F. Peel and quarter the potatoes and celeriac and place them in a large pot of salted water. Bring to a boil. Cook until the potatoes are tender when pierced with a fork, 12 to 15 minutes; the celeriac will be a little less tender. Drain in a colander. Return to the pan, add the milk, and mash with a potato masher. It's okay if the mixture is still a little lumpy. Reserve.

2. In a medium-sized saucepan, boil the water, butter, and salt. Add the flour all at once. Cook and stir the dough with a wooden spoon until it starts to pull away from the sides of the pan and begins to dry out a bit—approximately 3 minutes.

3. Put the dough in a medium-sized bowl and add the eggs. Using a hand mixer, beat until the eggs are incorporated into the dough.

4. Add the dough to the potato-celeriac mixture. Using a potato masher, mix the dough into the potato mixture.

5. Spray a baking dish large enough to handle the mixture with the baking spray. Coat with the breadcrumbs, reserving some for the top. Spread the potato-celeriac mixture in the dish. Coat the top with the remaining breadcrumbs and spray lightly with more baking spray.

6. Place in the oven and bake for 30 to 40 minutes, or until the top starts to brown.

Grilled Butterflied Leg of Lamb

According to the United States Department of Agriculture, lamb labeled "genuine lamb," "lamb," or "spring lamb" must be less than one year old and processed between the first Monday in March and the first Monday in October. In general, the paler the meat, the younger the lamb—and the more tender. Domestic lamb, which is usually grain-fed, tends to be more tender than imported, grass-fed lamb: look for a red, white, and blue sticker that says "Certified Fresh American Lamb." Remember that it takes time to properly butterfly a leg of lamb, so order it in advance. Count on ⅓ to ½ pound of meat per person.

1. With a sharp knife, make incisions across the top and bottom of the lamb that are deep enough to hold the garlic slivers. Insert a garlic sliver into each incision. Rub the lamb with the oil and then sprinkle it with the rosemary. Generously dust the lamb with salt and pepper. Wrap it in plastic wrap and refrigerate for an hour or so.

2. Remove the lamb from the refrigerator about 30 minutes prior to grilling. Ignite about 3 pounds of charcoal briquettes in a covered kettle grill. Once the coals are covered with a fine gray ash, arrange them in a single layer in the center of the grill. Put the cooking rack in place, 5 to 6 inches above the fire if you have an adjustable grill.

3. Place the lamb directly over the hot fire. If you are using a covered grill, put the lid in place, leaving the top and bottom vents completely open. Turn the lamb every 10 to 12 minutes. Move the meat away from the fire if it begins to char.

4. Total cooking time should be between 40 and 60 minutes, depending on your grill, the weather conditions, and the degree of doneness you desire. Using an instant-read thermometer, check the internal temperature of the lamb after it has been on the grill for 30 minutes or so. Lamb is rare at 140°F, medium at 160°F, and well-done at 170°F. Remember that the meat will continue to cook after it has been removed from the grill, so it's advisable to remove it from the heat when the temperature is about 5 degrees shy of the desired temperature.

5. Place the lamb on a cutting board and loosely tent it with foil; allow it to rest for 10 minutes or so before carving it against the grain. Serve overlapping slices on a larger platter topped with any leftover juices from the carving board and perhaps a garnish of fresh parsley or mint.

4- to 6-pound leg of lamb, boned and butterflied

2 to 3 garlic cloves, peeled and cut into 8 to 12 slivers total

2 tablespoons olive oil

1 teaspoon dried rosemary, crumbled

Kosher salt and freshly ground pepper to taste

Parsley or mint sprigs, for garnish, if desired

Tortilla Española

The name "Tortilla Española" confuses most folks. This Spanish favorite is essentially a potato and onion frittata and bears no resemblance to a Mexican tortilla. Like most popular home recipes, there are almost as many variations on this dish as there are cooks who make it. The most common addition is diced green pepper, added to the pan at the same time as the onions. The yield can be easily adjusted up or down. Just remember the Spanish rule of thumb: one egg per person, plus two for the pan. Try this dish once and it's certain to become a favorite in your house too.

4 tablespoons olive oil

½ medium onion, peeled and diced

6 medium potatoes, quartered lengthwise and thinly sliced (approximately 4 cups)

10 eggs

Kosher salt and freshly ground pepper to taste

1. Place 3 tablespoons of the oil and the diced onion in a 10-inch nonstick skillet over medium-high heat. Sauté the onions until just soft, about 5 minutes. Add the sliced potatoes and stir to coat them in oil. Cover the pan and cook until the potatoes are soft, stirring occasionally, 20 to 25 minutes. Reduce the heat if the onions begin to brown.

2. Whisk the eggs in a large bowl along with the salt and pepper. Add the cooked potato-onion mixture to the eggs, stirring gently to completely coat the vegetables.

3. Reduce the heat to low. Add the remaining tablespoon oil to the nonstick pan in which the potatoes and onions were cooked. Pour the egg-onion-potato mixture in the pan, spreading the mixture evenly. The eggs will begin to set at the edges almost immediately. Run a flexible, heat-resistant spatula around the edge of the tortilla, allowing the uncooked eggs to run under the cooked edges. Cook, covered, for 8 to 10 minutes. When done, the edges will be cooked but the center still runny.

4. Place a flat plate larger than the skillet upside down on top of the skillet. Holding the plate in place with one hand and the handle of the skillet with the other hand, flip the plate-covered skillet upside down. Gently slide the tortilla back into the pan and return it to the low heat. Using the spatula, tuck the edges under the tortilla. Cover and cook for approximately 10 minutes more. Press the center of the tortilla with the spatula; the tortilla will be done when the center is firm.

5. Slide the cooked tortilla onto a large plate and cut it into wedges. Serve hot, at room temperature, or cold.

Pasta with Prawns Piccata

This recipe was inspired by the famous Italian dish veal piccata, using its signature ingredients, lemon juice and capers. It's a great pasta for a crowd, it comes together literally in minutes, and it is very low in fat. Serve with some warm crusty bread and a green salad and you've got a fast feast.

1. Bring a large pot of salted water to a boil. Add the spaghetti and cook according to package instructions. When done, drain but do not rinse and return to the pot. Toss with 1 tablespoon of the oil. Set aside until the sauce is finished.

2. While the pasta is cooking, add the remaining 1 tablespoon of oil to a large sauté pan over medium-high heat. Add the shallots, bell pepper, and garlic. Sauté until just wilted, 5 to 7 minutes.

3. Add the clam juice, vermouth, parsley, capers, lemon juice, pepper, and salt to the pan. Bring to a boil and add the prawns all at once. Stir rapidly. The prawns are done as soon as they turn pink, 2 to 3 minutes. Do not be tempted to cook them longer; they will become tough.

4. Put the drained pasta in a large bowl with low sides. Pour the sauce over the pasta and serve it forth.

Wine Tip: We think you can go two different ways with the pasta and the prawns: King Estate Pinot Gris from Oregon for something luxurious or a Nero d'Avola from Sicily for something rustic. How are you feeling? Like a peasant or a prince?

2 pounds spaghetti

2 tablespoons olive oil

¾ cup chopped shallots (3 or 4 large shallots)

1 red bell pepper, seeded and diced

4 to 5 cloves garlic, minced or pushed through a garlic press

3 bottles (8 ounces each) clam juice

½ cup dry vermouth

¾ cup finely chopped curly parsley

5 tablespoons capers

Juice of 2 large lemons

Freshly ground pepper to taste

1½ teaspoons kosher salt, or to taste

2 pounds medium prawns (20 to 25 per pound), uncooked

Torta Rustica

All over Europe, pastry shops and bakeries offer some version of a pastry filled with vegetables, meat, and cheese. The Italians call them "torta," meaning a tart or pie. We call them lovely. This meatless version, with portobello mushrooms in the starring role, really makes an impression on a brunch table. You can roast all your vegetables the night before and even make the filling and the dough. In the morning all you have left to do is assemble and bake. Note: The following egg dough for the torta crust is from Viana La Place and Evan Kleiman's wonderful book *Cucina Fresca* (Harper & Row, 1985). We gratefully reprint it here with permission from the authors. The pepper-roasting method came from *Trattoria Cooking* by Patricia Wells.

---

1. Combine the flour, salt, and butter in a food processor fitted with a metal blade. Process with short pulses until the mixture is crumbly. Add the eggs and yolks with short pulses; do not overmix. Add the milk gradually, with short pulses, until the dough begins to clump. (You may not need it all.)

2. Gather the dough into a ball. Wrap it in plastic wrap and refrigerate for at least 1 hour or up to 3 days. When ready to roll the dough, place it on parchment, wax paper, aluminum foil, or plastic wrap to facilitate handling.

To roast the vegetables
1. Preheat the oven to 375°F. Seed and quarter the peppers. Put them in a baking dish and sprinkle them with the oil and salt. Cover the top of the pan with foil and roast until the peppers are tender, stirring once, about 40 minutes.

2. Place the mushrooms on a baking sheet with a lip and sprinkle them with the oil and salt. Roast for 20 minutes. They are done when they are just soft.

3. Take the mushroom caps, one at a time, and press them between two plates—tipping the plates sideways as you hold them over the sink—to remove excess moisture.

To assemble the torta
1. Preheat the oven to 350°F. In a large bowl, combine all the ingredients for the spinach filling.

(continued)

FOR THE DOUGH

4 cups all-purpose flour

1 teaspoon kosher salt

1 cup (2 sticks) cold unsalted butter, cut into pieces

2 eggs

2 egg yolks

1/3 cup milk

FOR THE ROASTED VEGETABLES

8 colored bell peppers, red, yellow, orange, or a combination

Olive oil to taste

Kosher salt to taste

6 large portobello mushrooms, stems removed

FOR THE SPINACH FILLING

2 pounds ricotta

4 eggs

1 cup grated Parmesan cheese

5 packages (10 ounces each) frozen spinach, defrosted and squeezed to remove excess moisture

1/2 cup golden raisins

FOR ASSEMBLING THE TORTA

1 pound Provolone cheese, sliced

3 cups artichoke hearts, drained

Egg wash (1 egg and 1 tablespoon cream, beaten together)

2. Roll out two-thirds of the dough into a large round. Line a round casserole, at least 3 inches deep and 12 inches across, with plastic wrap. Put the dough round on top of the plastic, fitting it into the shape of the casserole.

3. Spread a layer using half of the spinach filling, then a layer of all the roasted peppers on top of the dough. Continue with layers of half the cheese, all the roasted mushrooms, the remaining cheese, and the artichokes, ending with a layer of the spinach filling.

4. Roll out the remaining dough and fit it over the top of the torta. Fold the ends of the larger dough round over the top piece of dough to seal the torta, as now you are going to invert this masterpiece. First strengthen the seal at the edges with a little water if necessary.

5. You may want help with this part: Place a baking sheet with a lip on top of the casserole dish. With the baking sheet held firmly against the casserole dish, turn the torta upside down onto the baking sheet. Remove the casserole dish and the plastic wrap. Check the seal around the edges of the pastry, making sure it's good and closed.

6. Brush the top of the torta with the egg wash. Bake until the torta is golden brown, about 50 minutes. Remove it from the oven and let it cool.

7. This dish is perfect to serve at room temperature. After it has cooled down for 30 minutes or so, use two spatulas and a friend to slip it off the baking sheet and onto a big round platter.

Wine Tip: If this torta is part of a brunch menu, you might want to try a Moscato d'Asti for a real taste delight. If you are using it as a lunch or supper item, drink Chianti Classico.

Paella

Both Lou Jane and I have been making a variety of paellas for many years. Somehow, however, the fact that paella started as a dish cooked over an open fire was lost on us until we read the fabulous tome about the history of Spanish cuisine, *Culinaria Spain* (published by Konemann in Germany). "Could we cook it on the Weber grill?" Lou Jane asked. It wasn't long before we found a beautiful paellera 18 inches across, just right for the standard 22-inch Weber grill. We assembled the ingredients, started a fire, and we were off. Not only was there quite a bit of theater involved in the process, the finished product was delicious! If you don't have access to an outdoor fire, don't worry; paella tastes great when it is started on the stovetop and finished in the oven.

---

1. Preheat the oven to 350°F. Rinse the chicken pieces and pat them dry with paper towels. Roast the chicken in the oven until done, about 25 minutes, and set aside. You can do this several hours before, chill, and take the chicken out of the refrigerator when you start making the paella.

2. In a large saucepan, heat the chicken stock and white wine. In a dry sauté pan over medium heat, heat the saffron until it begins to have aroma, then add it to the stock. Add the paprika and stir. Keep warm.

3. In a large paella pan, Dutch oven, or baking pan, heat the oil over medium heat. Add the onion, garlic, and peppers and cook until the onion is soft, about 10 minutes. Add the rice and coat it with oil. With a soup ladle, add about 4 cups of the stock-wine combination to the rice mixture. Continue adding liquid 2 cups at a time. Stir often and allow the rice to absorb the liquid in between each addition.

4. After about 10 minutes, add the sausage, artichoke hearts, tomatoes with their juice, and garbanzo beans. Add the remaining liquid, a couple of ladles at a time, and stir continuously, as you would when making risotto.

5. When the rice is beginning to be tender, about 25 minutes, add the shrimp and scallops and the roasted chicken parts. Stir gently but not as often after you add the shrimp and scallops; they will fall apart with vigorous stirring.

6. After 5 minutes, add the mussels and peas and cover the pan for at least 5 minutes. When the rice is tender, the mussels *(continued)*

8 chicken drumsticks or thighs (1 per person)

1½ cups chicken stock per ½ cup of rice

2 cups white wine

1½ teaspoons saffron threads

1 tablespoon paprika

¼ cup olive oil

1 large onion, peeled and diced

6 cloves garlic, peeled and diced

1 each red and green bell pepper, seeded, quartered, and diced

½ cup uncooked rice per person, either Valencia or Bomba

1 pound smoked sausage, cut into 2-inch pieces

1 can (15 ounces) quartered artichoke hearts, drained

1 can (28 ounces) Italian tomatoes, undrained

1 can (15 ounces) garbanzo beans, drained

1 pound large uncooked shrimp, peels on

1 pound scallops, cleaned thoroughly

2 pounds mussels

1 package (10 ounces) frozen peas, defrosted

are open, and the shrimp are just cooked through, you have a paella. Transfer to a large bowl or a big platter with a lip, or serve the paella right out of the pan.

Variation: To make the paella on the stovetop, follow the directions in steps 1 through 4, cooking the ingredients over medium heat on the stovetop until it is time to add the shrimp, scallops, and chicken. Add all of them, along with the mussels and peas, cover the pan, and finish the paella in a 375°F oven. Stir every 7 to 10 minutes. The paella should be done in about 45 minutes.

Wine Tip: If your paella is part of an out-of-doors celebration, the Spanish Rosé from Rioja by Muga is a "one wine fits all" choice. If you want to go red and white, choose the delicious Albariño white from the Rias Baixas region and also a Spanish red. Maybe this is the time for Cellars Capcanes' yummy Mas Donis from Sicily.

Trout in Bondage

March 1 is opening day for trout season in Missouri. Hundreds of folks line the banks of the rivers in southern Missouri to fly fish, proof positive that hope springs eternal. Similar opening days occur across the country—annual events where, once again, humans try to outfox the wily trout. Here's a good recipe—even if you have to buy your trout from the grocery store.

8 to 12 boned whole trout (12 to 16 ounces each), 1 per person

16 to 24 strips bacon (2 per trout), for wrapping

FOR THE STUFFING

5 strips bacon, cooked crisp and crumbled, bacon grease reserved

1 small onion, peeled and diced

2 cups cooked rice

2 packages (10 ounces each) frozen chopped spinach, defrosted with warm running water and squeezed to remove most of the moisture

½ teaspoon kosher salt

¼ teaspoon each of dried dill and grated nutmeg

1. To make the stuffing, sauté the onion over low heat in the grease left from cooking the bacon until the onion is soft and just starting to brown, 5 to 7 minutes.

2. Remove from the heat and transfer the onion with the bacon fat into a bowl that contains the rice, spinach, crumbled bacon, salt, dill, and nutmeg. Stir to combine.

3. Stuff each trout with 2 to 5 tablespoons of the stuffing mixture, according to its size. Tie each one shut with 2 slices of raw bacon, one tied around the fish at the upper part of the body and the other piece tied around the fish toward the tail end.

4. Prepare a charcoal or gas-fired grill. Grill the trout directly over a hot fire, cooking for 10 minutes per inch of thickness. For example, a 1-inch-thick trout will take 10 minutes to cook—5 minutes per side. A small trout, say ¾ inch thick, will take approximately 7½ minutes to cook, a little over 3 minutes per side. Turn the fish only once, halfway through the total cooking time.

5. Place the fish on a large platter—a very impressive sight. Instruct diners to remove the bacon and then cut along the top of the trout's back, peeling the delectable fillet down, removing it from the bones. The bacon should be eaten along with the fillet.

Wine Tip: This is a classic combination of spinach, trout, and bacon. It deserves a classic German Riesling to drink with it.

Rabbit with Mustard Sauce

French bistro cooking is prevalent in America right now. We think it fits into our need for something full of flavor but not over-the-top fancy. If you haven't tried to cook rabbit before, this is an absolutely delicious way to start.

---

1. Season the rabbit with salt and pepper. In a heavy Dutch oven or deep frying pan, heat 3 tablespoons of the oil to medium heat and brown the rabbit pieces on all sides, about 12 minutes. Set aside.

2. Add the extra tablespoon of oil to the pan you've used to brown the rabbit and sauté the onion, garlic, and shallots. After 5 to 7 minutes, deglaze the pan with ⅓ cup cognac.

3. Return the rabbit pieces to the pan along with the wine, stock, mustard, and rosemary. Cover and cook over medium-low heat, 30 to 45 minutes, until the rabbit is tender.

4. Remove the rabbit to a big platter, cook down the sauce until it thickens, 5 to 10 minutes, add the cream and the remaining cognac, and remove from the heat. Pour the sauce over the rabbit. Top with the parsley and serve immediately.

Wine Tip: This French rabbit dish is rich enough in cream to pair with a French Bordeaux Supérieure with all its fat-cutting tannins. Or go for something higher up the totem pole if you can afford it.

2 rabbits (about 5 pounds total), cut into 6 pieces each (ask the butcher to do this)

Kosher salt and freshly ground pepper

4 tablespoons canola oil

1 large onion, peeled and diced

3 to 6 cloves garlic, peeled and sliced

4 shallots, peeled and diced

⅓ cup cognac plus ¼ cup for the sauce

1 bottle (750 ml) white wine

1 cup chicken stock

⅓ cup Dijon mustard

2 tablespoons dried rosemary

1⅓ cups heavy cream

½ cup Italian (flat-leaf) parsley leaves

Grilled Tuna with White Beans and Basil Oil

Many years ago we visited a good friend at his home up the California coast. He wasn't exactly known for his culinary skills, but this day found him uncharacteristically focused in the kitchen. Seems he had just returned from Tuscany and was eager to recreate a dish he had tasted there: an unlikely combination of marinated white beans and canned tuna. It was hard, at that point, to imagine a more misguided effort, but the day was warm and beautiful, the view of the Pacific through the pines engaging, and the white wine perfectly chilled. By the time we had our first bite, we knew we had encountered something extraordinary. Over the years we've modified the recipe, primarily by replacing the canned tuna with fresh grilled tuna and coming up with our own basil-infused dressing. This is darn near the perfect room-temperature Big Platter dish, just the thing for an al fresco lunch.

1. To make the bean salad, soak and simmer the beans according to package directions and drain. Combine the cooked beans with all the peppers, onion, and parsley. Season the beans with salt and pepper and toss with the oil and vinegar. Let set for an hour before serving or make this the night before and adjust the seasonings at serving time. You will probably need to add a little more oil, as the beans absorb it, as well as additional salt and pepper.

2. Rinse the tuna in cold water and dry it with a paper towel. Rub a little vegetable oil onto both sides of the tuna and dust it with white pepper and salt to taste.

3. Prepare a charcoal or gas-fired grill. Grill the tuna steaks directly over a moderately hot fire for approximately 5 minutes per side, turning once halfway through the cooking process. The fish is done when it's still slightly pink at the center; take a peek with a sharp knife to be sure. Once cooked, remove the steaks from the grill and reserve on a plate, loosely tented with foil.

4. Put the pine nuts in a dry sauté pan over medium heat. Shake the pan frequently to prevent burning. Watch carefully; remove when just lightly browned, about 5 minutes.

5. To make the dressing, put the basil leaves in a food processor, turn it on, and drizzle in the oil, scraping down the sides of the processor once. Season with kosher salt. Reserve until needed, but not longer than 30 minutes.

6. Using a slotted spoon, put the beans on a large platter in an even layer. Break up the grilled tuna into chunks, *(continued)*

FOR THE BEAN SALAD
1 pound dried white beans

1 red bell pepper, seeded and diced

1 orange bell pepper, seeded and diced

1 yellow bell pepper, seeded and diced

1 red onion, peeled and diced

1 cup chopped Italian (flat-leaf) parsley

Kosher salt and freshly ground pepper to taste

3/4 cup extra-virgin olive oil

1/3 cup red wine vinegar or sherry vinegar

FOR THE TUNA AND GARNISHES
4 to 5 tuna steaks (about 2 to 3 pounds), approximately 1 inch thick

Vegetable oil

Ground white pepper and kosher salt to taste

1 cup pine nuts

2 ripe tomatoes, sliced into wedges

2 lemons, cut into wedges

Black olives, the small niçoise type, if you can find them

FOR THE DRESSING

1 cup fresh basil leaves

½ cup olive oil

Kosher salt to taste

approximately 1½ to 2 inches in diameter, and place them on top of the beans. Pour the basil dressing over the top of the tuna and allow it to spill onto the beans. Garnish the platter with the toasted pine nuts, tomatoes, lemons, and olives.

Wine Tip: We think tuna shows much better with a red wine than a white, so we'd look to Pinot Noirs from the Russian River appellation of California and do a little taste-testing. Buy from a couple of different producers and see what you think.

"Ladies Who Lunch" Luncheon

Everyone needs a special lunch menu now and then: your college roommates have come to town, the in-laws are visiting, your best friend's daughter got engaged. Whatever it is, it's an event that requires fresh flowers, your best china and flatware, and fuss-free food that seems like you've been fussing a lot.

§ Green Bean Salad with Hazelnuts
§ Chicken Crêpes with Sauce Royale
§ Frozen Fruit Salad
§ Butterscotch and Baileys Trifle (page 179)

Wine Tip: There is nothing wrong with the cliché in this case. Ladies Who Lunch love Chardonnay. Give them the best you can afford. The creamier, the better.

Green Bean Salad with Hazelnuts

We know the Ladies Who Lunch don't like green lettuce salads served buffet style. These salads flop all over your plate and can be very messy. Spring is the prime time for green beans so they are a wonderful substitute for a lettuce-based salad.

1. Blanch the green beans in a stockpot of boiling water for 2 to 5 minutes. Remove from the heat, drain in a colander, and plunge the beans in a bowl of ice water. Let them stand in the ice water until you are ready to proceed with the salad.

2. When ready, drain the green beans and dry them, laying them between two cloth tea towels to absorb the water. When they are dry, line up the beans in neat piles and cut them into 2-inch pieces.

3. To make the dressing, place the shallot, mustard, and vinegar in a food processor or blender. Turn it on and drizzle in the oil, stopping the motor at least once to wipe down the sides of the bowl.

4. In a large mixing bowl, combine the green beans and the chopped nuts with the salt and pepper. Toss with the dressing and turn out on a platter with a lip or a shallow bowl. This salad can be made 2 to 4 hours ahead of time without the nuts. Just add the nuts near serving time so they don't get soggy.

2 pounds green beans

1½ cups hazelnuts, toasted and coarsely chopped (see page 18)

1 teaspoon kosher salt

½ teaspoon freshly ground pepper

FOR THE DRESSING
1 shallot, peeled and halved

¼ cup each of Dijon mustard and coarse ground mustard

⅓ cup sherry vinegar

1 cup walnut or hazelnut oil

Chicken Crêpes with Sauce Royale

Long ago in Kansas City there was a fancy restaurant on the Plaza named Putsch's 210. These are our approximation of their chicken crêpes, which were a favorite of both the ladies and men who lunched there. This recipe makes 18 to 20 crêpes.

FOR THE CRÊPES

1⅓ cups milk

1 cup all-purpose flour

1 tablespoon sugar

3 eggs

¼ teaspoon kosher salt

3 tablespoons melted butter

Canola oil, for the pan

A crêpe pan or small sauté pan

FOR THE FILLING

5 pounds bone-in chicken breasts

1 carrot, washed but unpeeled

Tops and bottom of a head of celery

5 stalks celery, sliced thin

1 can (8 ounces) water chestnuts, drained and chopped into small dice

2 cups slivered almonds, lightly toasted

1 cup grated Monterey Jack cheese

1 cup sour cream

1 teaspoon each of kosher salt, ground white pepper, paprika, celery seed, and dried dill

Juice of 1 lemon

Nonstick baking spray

1 recipe Sauce Royale (recipe follows)

⅓ cup grated Parmesan cheese, to top the baked crêpes

1. To make the crêpes, mix together the milk, flour, sugar, eggs, and salt. Let the batter stand at least an hour. Right before you make the crêpes, add the melted butter.

2. Heat a crêpe pan over medium heat. Dampen a paper towel with canola oil and wipe the pan with it to lightly grease it. Using a small ladle (a 1½-ounce one if available), ladle a small amount of batter into the pan. Swirl it around quickly to cover the bottom of the pan. Cook for about 2 minutes, then turn over using a spatula and cook another minute, until the crêpe is set. Turn it out on wax paper.

3. Repeat until you've used all the batter. You can make them a day ahead; wrap them tightly in plastic wrap and store in the refrigerator.

4. To make the filling, rinse the chicken breasts and put them in a large stockpot with enough cold water to cover. Add the carrot and the tops and bottom of the celery. Bring to a boil and simmer until the breasts are cooked through, 20 to 30 minutes. Drain, reserving the stock, and cool.

5. When the chicken is cool enough to handle, pull all the meat from the bones and dice it. Put it in a large bowl and add the celery, water chestnuts, almonds, cheese, sour cream, salt, pepper, paprika, celery seed, dill, and lemon juice. You can do this much the night before; just cover and refrigerate.

6. Preheat the oven to 350°F. When you are ready to assemble the crêpes, place a couple of tablespoons of the chicken mixture on the upper third of a crêpe. Roll it up and place it in a shallow baking dish that has been sprayed with baking spray. Repeat until you have filled and rolled all the crêpes. Cover the crêpes with aluminum foil and bake them for 25 minutes, or until they are heated through.

7. Uncover and top the crêpes with the Sauce Royale (reserve some for serving if you like) and Parmesan. Bake until the top is browned and the sauce is bubbling, about 20 minutes. Arrange the hot crêpes on a big platter and top with the rest of the sauce.

Sauce Royale

In a heavy saucepan over medium heat, melt the butter and stir in the flour. Cook for 3 to 5 minutes to make a light golden roux. Add the stock and cream. Whisk to blend thoroughly. Reduce heat to low and cook until the sauce starts to thicken. Add ½ cup Parmesan and simmer for another 5 minutes. This sauce can be made ahead of time and reheated.

2 tablespoons butter

2 tablespoons all-purpose flour

1½ cups chicken stock, reserved from cooking the chicken breasts

1½ cups heavy cream or half-and-half

½ cup grated Parmesan cheese

Frozen Fruit Salad

This salad idea is so "out" that it can't be long before it's "in" again. In or out, it sure tastes good. Lou Jane got this recipe from her mother, who got it from her sister-in-law in the 1950s, when it was considered very chic.

Line a loaf pan with plastic wrap so it extends 3 inches beyond each end. Combine all the ingredients and transfer the mixture to the prepared pan. Freeze for 4 to 6 hours or overnight, until the salad is frozen through. To serve, use the ends of the plastic wrap to lift the salad out of the loaf pan; invert on a big platter, wait 5 minutes, then peel off the plastic.

2 cups sour cream

¾ cup sugar

2 tablespoons lemon juice

¼ teaspoon kosher salt

½ cup lightly toasted walnuts, chopped

3 tablespoons chopped maraschino cherries

1 can (9 ounces) crushed pineapple, drained

1 banana, peeled and diced

1 teaspoon vanilla extract

Snapper à la Veracruzana

When you go to a place like Acapulco or Cancun or Cabo San Lucas, having a whole snapper at a beach restaurant is a must-do dining experience. With this great recipe, you can have the same taste treat in your own backyard without the sand in your sauce!

---

1. To make the sauce, heat the olive oil in a medium saucepan over medium heat. Add the onion and garlic and sauté until the onion wilts and is translucent, about 7 minutes. Add the tomatoes, jalapeños, olives, cinnamon, cloves, sugar, lemon juice, and salt and stir to combine. Simmer over low heat for 10 minutes. Stir in the capers and remove from the heat. Cover until the fish is grilled.

2. Prepare a hot charcoal or gas-fired grill. Rinse the whole snapper in cold water and pat dry with paper towels. Rub liberally with the oil and sprinkle, inside and out, with the salt and pepper. Grill the snapper directly over a moderately hot fire for a total cooking time of 20 to 25 minutes, turning the fish every 5 to 7 minutes. The fish is done when the flesh is just uniformly white and measures at least 140°F on an instant-read thermometer. (If using an instant-read thermometer, be sure to insert it in the thickest part of the fish, without touching the bone.)

3. While the fish is grilling, reheat the sauce. Remove the snapper from the grill and place it in the middle of a large platter. Top with the sauce. Garnish with lemon slices and chopped fresh cilantro, if desired.

Wine Tip: You have to look to Italy for wine to go with grilled fish that also has a flavorful tomato-based sauce. Monte Antico is an inexpensive Tuscan wine that really delivers for the money. Mexican beer would be delicious as well.

1 whole red snapper (4 pounds or less)

Vegetable oil

Kosher salt and freshly ground pepper

FOR THE SAUCE
¼ cup olive oil

1 large onion, peeled and diced

3 to 6 cloves garlic, peeled and minced

8 tomatoes (3 to 4 pounds) chopped, or
    4 tomatoes and 1 large can (28 ounces)
    whole Italian tomatoes, undrained

3 fresh jalapeño peppers, seeded and diced

8 ounces green olives stuffed with
    pimentos, drained and halved

½ teaspoon cinnamon

¼ teaspoon ground cloves

1 teaspoon sugar

Juice of 1 lemon

1 teaspoon kosher salt

2 tablespoons capers, drained

Lemon slices and chopped fresh cilantro,
    for garnish (optional)

Duck Breast with Fresh Figs and Port

Prepare this dish and you'll instantly gain celebrity status as a chef—it's that impressive and delicious. It is a rich and full-flavored meal, perfect for special occasions. You can, of course, make your own demi-glace (provided you have several days and 15 or so pounds of beef and veal bones), but luckily this intense reduced stock is now available in jars or in the frozen food section of many supermarkets.

---

1 quart fresh ripe figs

2 cups port

8 Pekin (Long Island) duck breasts, cut in half (about 4 pounds total)

1 tablespoon olive oil

1 cup prepared demi-glace

½ teaspoon dried rosemary, crumbled

1. Start this dish the night before by piercing the fresh figs in several places with a skewer. Place them in a glass jar just large enough to hold them snugly. Add the port to completely cover the figs. Cover and refrigerate until needed.

2. Using a sharp knife, score the duck skin approximately ⅛-inch deep in a crisscross pattern.

3. Heat the oil, over medium-high heat, in a heavy sauté pan large enough to hold the duck breasts. Place the breasts skin side down and cook for approximately 4 minutes; turn and cook for another 2 minutes for medium-rare duck. Remove the breasts from the pan, place on a platter, and loosely tent with foil.

4. Pour off the fat from the sauté pan. Pour the port from the marinating figs into the pan. Bring it to a boil and reduce the liquid by half. Once reduced, add the demi-glace and reduce the heat to medium-high. Cook for 2 minutes.

5. Cut the figs in half lengthwise. Add them to the port mixture, along with the rosemary. Cook an additional 2 minutes.

6. Cut each of the duck breasts on the bias into three slices. Place the slices on a large platter, surround them with the fig halves, and strain the hot sauce over the top. Serve immediately.

Wine Tip: Again, we would look to Pinot Noir for a match to this dish. A French Burgundy or Carneros Pinot Noir from California should suit the elegance of the duck.

Indian food is still considered slightly exotic in America. That makes it a perfect cuisine to surprise your friends and family with at home. Pulling off a whole home-style Indian meal is much easier than you would think. Most of the spices of the world are at your fingertips locally, or you can order them online.

§ **Tandoori Chicken**

§ **Shrimp Vindaloo**

§ **Spicy Eggplant**

§ **Sesame Rice**

§ **Cucumber Raita**

§ **Kalan**

§ **Pappadums**

Wine Tip: In the old days of winemaking in Alsace, they blended all five of their local varietals together: Sylvaner, Gewürztraminer, Pinot Gris, Muscat, and Riesling. The winery Hugel does this today under the name Gentil. Try it.

Tandoori **Chicken**

The word "tandoori" actually refers to a top-loading brick and clay oven (called a tandoor), traditionally found throughout India. Food is cooked directly over a hot, smoky fire inside the oven where temperatures can reach 500°F or more. Although the results will not be identical, cooking this flavorful chicken directly over a charcoal or gas flame can produce an excellent meal. Serve with your favorite chutney, if so desired.

1. Rinse the chicken pieces and pat them dry with paper towels. Using a sharp knife, diagonally slash the chicken pieces about ¼ inch deep to allow the marinade to penetrate the meat.

2. Combine all the marinade ingredients. Taste and adjust seasoning, keeping in mind that the strength of the cayenne will increase after an hour or so.

3. Place the chicken in a large Ziploc bag or container with a lid. Pour the marinade over the chicken, making sure all the pieces are coated. Refrigerate for at least 4 hours, preferably overnight.

4. Remove the chicken from the refrigerator about 30 minutes before grilling. Prepare a charcoal or gas-fired grill.

5. Grill the chicken over a moderately hot fire, turning the chicken pieces every 7 minutes or so, and basting with the melted butter each time. Total cooking time will be between 20 and 30 minutes.

6 to 8 pounds boneless, skinless chicken breasts or bone-in, skinless thighs, or a combination of the two

⅓ cup melted butter

FOR THE MARINADE

2 tablespoons each of finely chopped garlic and finely chopped fresh ginger

½ cup peanut oil or other vegetable oil

1 teaspoon ground turmeric

¼ teaspoon cayenne, or more to taste

1 cup plain yogurt

1 teaspoon kosher salt

Shrimp Vindaloo

Vindaloo is one of the Indian preparations that has become popular in America. Shrimp lends itself to this spicy vinegar bath very nicely.

1 teaspoon ground cumin

2 teaspoons mustard seeds

½ teaspoon turmeric

1 teaspoon each of ground cardamom, ground cinnamon, cayenne, and kosher salt

4 cloves garlic, peeled and halved

1-inch piece of ginger, peeled and sliced

2 onions, one peeled and cut into chunks and one peeled and sliced

½ cup white vinegar

1 teaspoon brown sugar

2 pounds large uncooked shrimp, peeled and deveined

3 tablespoons canola oil

1½ pounds tomatoes, chopped, or 1 large can (28 ounces) Italian-style chopped tomatoes

1 pound red potatoes, cooked and diced

1. In a dry sauté pan over medium-high heat, heat the cumin, mustard seeds, turmeric, cardamom, cinnamon, cayenne, and salt until the mustard seeds start to pop and you can smell them. Do not breathe in the fumes, as mustard gas is extremely potent.

2. In a food processor or blender, combine the spices you just heated, along with the garlic, ginger, chunks of onion, vinegar, and brown sugar. Process into a puree.

3. In a large covered bowl or Ziploc bag, combine the shrimp and the puree. Marinate for at least 1 hour but not more than 3 hours, as the acid in the vinegar will start to "cook" the shrimp.

4. In a large sauté pan or saucepan, heat the canola oil over medium heat. Add the sliced onion and sauté. When the onion is soft and starting to brown, add the tomatoes and potatoes. Cook for about 5 minutes then add the shrimp and the marinade. Cook until the shrimp have turned pink and the mixture is heated through, about 10 minutes. Do not overcook, as the shrimp will begin to toughen.

Spicy Eggplant

If yours is a meatless household, you can have a wonderful feast using the next four recipes. Although there are probably hundreds of Indian recipes for eggplant, we like this one because it calls for slicing the eggplant lengthwise, which gives it a different finished character, and also because of the texture of the grated coconut.

1. Toast the sesame seeds by spreading them on a baking sheet and roasting them in a preheated 325°F oven until lightly brown, about 10 minutes.

2. In a large sauté pan, heat 2 tablespoons of the oil over medium-high heat and brown the eggplant slices in batches, setting them aside on paper towels to drain. You will have to add more oil as you go, as the eggplant will absorb the oil quickly.

3. Heat another 2 to 3 tablespoons of the oil in the same pan. Fry the coriander, chili powder, turmeric, mustard seeds, garlic, and onions until the onions are soft, 5 to 7 minutes. Add the grated coconut, lemon, toasted sesame seeds, jalapeño, brown sugar, water, salt, and bay leaf to the spicy onions. Add the browned eggplant. Cover and simmer until the eggplant is tender, about 20 minutes. Garnish with cilantro leaves, if desired.

1/4 cup sesame seeds

About 1/2 cup canola oil

3 eggplants (about 3 pounds total), trimmed and sliced thinly lengthwise

1 tablespoon ground coriander

1 teaspoon chili powder

1/2 teaspoon turmeric

1 teaspoon mustard seeds

6 cloves garlic, peeled and sliced

3 onions, peeled and sliced

1/2 cup grated unsweetened coconut

Juice and pulp of 2 lemons

1 fresh jalapeño pepper, quartered, seeded, and sliced

1 tablespoon brown sugar

1 cup water

1 teaspoon kosher salt

1 bay leaf

Fresh cilantro leaves, for garnish (optional)

Sesame Rice

You could use plain fragrant rice with your Indian menu, but this is so easy and tastes so good, it's worth an extra step. You can make this dish an hour or so ahead of time.

4 cups water

2½ cups uncooked basmati rice

¼ cup clarified butter or canola oil

⅓ cup cashew nuts

2 tablespoons sesame seeds

½ teaspoon cayenne

1 teaspoon kosher salt

Juice of 1 lime

1. Heat the 4 cups water to a boil in a medium saucepan with a lid. Add the rice. Reduce the heat to low and cover. Simmer until the water is absorbed, about 20 minutes. Remove the pan from the heat and set it aside, letting it stand covered for at least another 5 to 10 minutes.

2. Heat the butter or oil in a large sauté pan over medium heat. Add the cashews, sesame seeds, cayenne, and salt and let the sesame seeds and nuts lightly brown, 5 to 6 minutes. Combine this mixture with the cooked rice and the lime juice and mound it on a large platter. Serve hot or at room temperature.

Cucumber Raita

Raita's purpose in an Indian meal is to serve as a cool contrast to the predominant hot and spicy flavors. To this end, we usually don't add the raw onion, but since it shows up in many raita combinations, we've made it an option.

2 cups plain yogurt

1 tablespoon honey

Pinch of cayenne

1 cucumber, seeded and diced

½ cup diced onion (optional)

Combine all ingredients and chill for at least 1 hour before serving.

Kalan

Kalan is another version of the palate-cooling Raita, but this one transcends condiment status—it's a dish in itself.

---

1. Peel the bananas and cut them into 1-inch-thick slices.

2. In a saucepan, combine the turmeric, bananas, water, and jalapeño. Cook over medium heat until the bananas are tender and the water has been absorbed, about 15 minutes. Remove from the heat.

3. In a sauté pan, heat the oil over medium heat and sauté the onion until brown, about 10 minutes. Remove from the heat.

4. In a dry sauté pan over medium-high heat, heat the pepper, cumin, mustard seeds, fenugreek, salt, and cayenne until the seeds start to pop and the mixture starts to smell spicy. Remember not to inhale over the spice pan as the fumes are very strong.

5. In a large bowl, combine the banana mixture, sautéed onion, toasted spices, yogurt, and grated coconut. Let the mixture stand at least 2 hours before serving. Serve at room temperature.

3 medium-ripe bananas (approximately 1 pound total)

1 teaspoon turmeric

⅓ cup water

1 fresh jalapeño pepper, seeded and minced

2 tablespoons canola oil

1 small onion, peeled and sliced

½ teaspoon freshly ground pepper

½ cup ground cumin

1 teaspoon mustard seeds

½ teaspoon fenugreek

1 teaspoon kosher salt

¼ teaspoon cayenne

2 cups plain yogurt

⅓ cup grated unsweetened coconut

Pappadums

These wafer-thin disks are made from lentil flour. Available at all Indian grocery stores, they come in various flavors: red pepper, garlic, and black pepper to name a few. Just heat about ¼-inch of peanut oil in a sauté pan and fry the pappadums a few seconds on each side. They'll puff up to double their original size. Lean them against a bowl in a stack and drain them onto a paper towel.

Spring Mushroom Risotto

If you are lucky enough to get your hands on some morels, this is a lovely way to use them. Pea shoots have become available at many farmers' markets around the country and contribute a unique taste. Crunchy and green, they seem to have the flavor of spring, if there is such a thing. Don't despair if you can't find them. Just use some flat-leaf parsley to decorate the top of the dish instead.

---

7 tablespoons butter

1 pound morels or white button mushrooms if morels are unavailable

½ pound shiitake mushrooms

2 tablespoons olive oil

1 sweet onion, such as Vidalia, peeled and diced

6 baby turnips, cleaned and diced

2 cups Arborio rice

2 to 3 quarts liquid, which can be white wine, chicken stock, Knorr mushroom cubes dissolved in water, or a combination

½ ounce dried porcini soaked in 2 cups warm water

1 pound sugar snap peas, blanched, or 2 pounds English peas, shelled

¾ cup grated Parmesan cheese

1 cup pea shoots or flat-leaf parsley, for garnish

1. In a large sauté pan, heat 3 tablespoons of the butter over low heat. Sauté the morels and shiitake mushrooms for about 12 minutes, or until their moisture is released and reduced to very little. Set aside.

2. In a second large, heavy sauté pan, heat 2 tablespoons of the butter and the oil over low heat. Add the onion and turnips and sauté them until the onions are soft, about 6 minutes. Add the rice and stir to coat it with the oil.

3. In a large saucepan, heat the liquids until simmering. Add a ladleful at a time to just cover the rice, onions, and turnips. Simmer, stirring, until the moisture has been absorbed by the rice. The amount of moisture needed to cook the rice will depend on the moisture content of the rice and vegetables.

4. When the rice is just beginning to soften, after about 15 minutes, add the sautéed mushrooms and the porcini. You can include some of the porcini soaking water—just make sure you don't tip the whole contents of the bowl into the risotto, as there will be sand or dirt at the bottom. Add the sugar snap peas. When the rice is cooked through but still firm, stir in the Parmesan cheese and the last 2 tablespoons butter. Turn onto a big platter and garnish with the pea shoots.

Wine Tip: Try a Valpolicella Ripasso from the Veneto region.

Big Platter Summer

What could be more fun than cooking for your friends and family in the summer? There are so many excuses to get together: long weekends abound, vacations are enjoyed, the garden starts yielding, the first good corn on the cob appears at the farmers' market. Then there's a party for your best friend's daughter on her wedding weekend, a celebration of the moment, even if it's only a lazy Sunday afternoon around the grill in the backyard. Food helps you grab summer while you can. It'll be September before you know it.

Fried Green Tomatoes with Shrimp Rémoulade

In New Orleans, you would never find roasted peppers in a rémoulade salad. The peppers are an addition from two cooks who aren't bound to the "classical New Orleans" tradition. The sweetness of the peppers is a nice contrast to the mustard and horseradish in the sauce. If green tomatoes are not available, the shrimp rémoulade is delicious on top of a bed of fresh baby spinach.

FOR THE FRIED TOMATOES

6 to 8 green tomatoes (about 3 pounds)

1 quart buttermilk, for soaking the tomatoes

2 to 3 cups flour seasoned to taste with kosher salt, ground cumin, and ground white pepper

Canola oil, for frying

Kosher salt, for sprinkling

FOR THE SHRIMP RÉMOULADE

2 pounds large shrimp, cooked, cleaned, and chopped into a large dice

2 each red and yellow bell peppers, roasted and diced (see Note)

1/2 to 1 cup mayonnaise

1/4 cup Creole or other spicy mustard

1/4 cup Dijon mustard

2 tablespoons horseradish

Juice of 1 lemon

1/2 teaspoon paprika

1/4 teaspoon cayenne

1/2 teaspoon each of kosher salt and freshly ground pepper

1 bunch green onions, sliced just into the green part

1. To make the rémoulade, combine the cooked shrimp with all of the other ingredients. Chill for at least an hour or up 6 hours. You can make the rémoulade long before you fry the tomatoes.

2. To prepare the fried tomatoes, cut the tomatoes into slices about 1/4 inch thick. Pour some of the buttermilk (enough to cover the tomatoes) into a shallow dish (such as a 9 x 1-inch baking dish) and add the tomato slices to the buttermilk to soak for 20 to 30 minutes. Place the seasoned flour in another shallow pan.

3. Heat the canola oil in a sauté pan over medium heat. Remove the tomato slices from the buttermilk and dredge them in the flour. Fry them in the oil, 3 to 5 minutes on each side, until they are browned. Drain on a paper towel and sprinkle with a little kosher salt.

4. Spread out the fried tomato slices on a big platter and top each with a spoonful of the rémoulade. Serve at room temperature.

Note: To prepare the roasted peppers, seed and quarter the peppers. Put them in a shallow baking dish, drizzle them with olive oil, and sprinkle with kosher salt. Cover with foil and bake at 350°F for 40 minutes, or until the peppers are tender, turning the peppers and checking their progress once. Remove from the oven and leave the foil on for 10 minutes, then remove it and let the peppers cool off. Peel off and discard the skins before chopping.

Wine Tip: The green tomatoes' acidity calls for a high-acidity wine. We found the most wonderful all-purpose summer wine that will go down very well with the shrimp and the bite of the green tomatoes. It's a dry Spanish Rosé from the Rioja district called Muga, delicious and inexpensive.

Lamb Kabobs

It wouldn't be summer without grilling some combination of meat and vegetables on a stick. The green olives and dates are an unusual pairing of salty and sweet that really complements and contrasts with the lamb. Count on two or three pieces of meat on each skewer, along with the alternating stuffed dates and zucchini.

¾ cup soy sauce

1½ cups sherry

1½ teaspoons ground ginger

1 teaspoon crushed red pepper flakes

9 cloves garlic, peeled and pushed through a garlic press

3 pounds leg of lamb or lamb stew meat, cut into 1-inch chunks

About 32 dates, enough for 16 kabobs

32 pitted green olives

6 zucchini, cut into 2-inch chunks

1. In a large bowl or Ziploc bag, combine the soy sauce, sherry, ginger, red pepper flakes, and garlic. Add the lamb and marinate for at least 4 hours. This can be done the night before you are using it.

2. When you are ready to assemble the kabobs, pit the dates and stuff them with the green olives. Alternate lamb, dates, and zucchini chunks on the skewers.

3. Prepare a charcoal or gas-fired grill. Grill the kabobs directly over the hot fire for approximately 10 minutes, 5 minutes per side, turning once. This will produce medium-rare lamb; adjust the cooking time by a minute or two for lamb that is rarer or more well done.

Wine Tips: We've created quite an array of tastes with the lamb, the green olives, and the dates. How about a northern Rhône like Cornas? Which leads us to another suggestion: Syrah. There are some very good ones in California now. We've already mentioned Qupe, and there's Edmunds St. John and Babcock as well.

Heartland Grain Salad

The nutty taste of wheat berries is a true revelation, so the goal of this salad is to let the taste of the individual grains shine. The salad can be dressed up to entree status with the addition of sliced, cooked chicken breasts, prawns, artichoke hearts, or a combination or used as a side dish to all kinds of braised meats such as North Beach Veal Stew (page 92) or Moroccan Chicken (page 50).

1. Cook the rice, barley, wheat berries, and soybeans separately according to their package directions.

2. Chop the dried fruits to similar bite-sized pieces. Lightly toast the seeds and nuts by placing them all on a baking sheet in a preheated 325°F oven for 10 minutes. In a large bowl, combine the cooked grains, dried fruits, and toasted seeds and nuts with the salt, pepper, and parsley. Toss with the oil and vinegar.

3. Let the salad rest at least an hour before serving. Taste at that time and add more oil, vinegar, or seasonings if needed. The grains tend to absorb moisture so you usually will have to add a little more oil and vinegar.

Variations: Substituting other oils and vinegars in this salad makes a tremendous difference in taste. A good cold-press olive oil works well, as does hazelnut oil. Try using rice wine vinegar, tarragon vinegar, or malt vinegar instead of the balsamic.

1 cup each of uncooked jasmine or basmati rice, barley, wheat berries, and soybeans

1½ cups dried fruit: your choice of a combination of apricots, dates, prunes, cranberries, raisins, and figs

1½ cups seeds and nuts: your choice of a combination of sesame seeds, sunflower seeds, pumpkin seeds, walnuts, almonds, peanuts, and hazelnuts

1½ teaspoons kosher salt

1 teaspoon ground white pepper

1 bunch curly parsley, rinsed, drained, and finely chopped

1½ cups each of walnut oil and balsamic vinegar, or more if needed

Steak with Salsa Verde

The term salsa verde throws people off, as they are probably more familiar with the Mexican salsa made from tomatillos than they are with this Italian sauce of the same name. Yes, both are green, but that's about where the similarity ends. The Italian version is a delightfully potent concoction of parsley, garlic, and other goodies, just right for standing up to the flavor of grilled steak. If you need a special meal in a hurry, this is it. If there's no time or inclination to fire up the grill, this steak is just as good done indoors on a hot cast-iron skillet.

---

4 to 5 pounds London broil, hanger, or flat-iron steaks (usually 2 steaks), cut 1 to 1½ inches thick

Olive oil to taste

Kosher salt and freshly ground pepper to taste

1 recipe Salsa Verde (recipe follows)

1. Prepare a charcoal or gas-fired grill. Rub the steak, top and bottom, with oil, salt, and plenty of freshly ground pepper. Let it sit at room temperature while the coals get hot.

2. For a medium-rare steak, grill over a hot fire for 5 minutes per side per inch of thickness. If the steak is cut 1½ inches thick, count on approximately 7 minutes a side.

3. Allow the steaks to rest for 5 to 10 minutes. Using a sharp butcher knife, carve the steak into ⅜-inch-thick slices. Place overlapping slices of steak on a platter and pour a "stripe" of salsa verde down the middle. Put the remaining sauce in a bowl for those who want seconds.

Salsa Verde

4 to 5 cups fresh parsley leaves, rinsed and patted dry

4 to 6 cloves peeled garlic, depending on your taste

Juice of 1 lemon and some of the pulp, if you can coax it out

2 tablespoons capers

2 teaspoons anchovy paste (optional)

½ cup olive oil

Place everything in a food processor or blender and process until your sauce is the consistency of a milkshake. Because of the salty nature of the capers and anchovies, no salt is needed.

Wine Tip: Cabernet Sauvignon from Napa Valley. With this simple dish, you can really show off some good bottles of what this region does so well: make world-class Cabernet Sauvignons.

Summer's End Ratatouille, Two Ways

Few recipes are better at using up great quantities of garden produce than ratatouille. Originating in the Provence region of France, there are almost as many versions of this dish—basically a vegetable stew—as there are cooks. For that reason, approximate amounts are given in the following "recipe." Feel free to alter those amounts depending on what your garden or farmers' market has to offer. Excellent hot, room temperature, or cold, ratatouille can also be served over pasta for a delicious vegetarian entree. And like so many stews, ratatouille is actually better the day after it's prepared.

We offer two versions: the first is the traditional stovetop version; the second is a grilled recipe.

Traditional Ratatouille

Extra-virgin olive oil (approximately 1/4 cup)

Yellow or white onions, coarsely chopped (approximately 1 1/2 cups)

3 or more cloves fresh garlic, peeled and finely chopped

Zucchini or crookneck squash, cut into 3/8-inch-thick slices, or pattypans, cut into even wedges (approximately 1 pound)

2 (more or less) bell peppers (in multiple colors, if possible), seeded and cut into 1-inch squares

2 (more or less) medium eggplants, peeled and cut into 1-inch cubes

5 (more or less) tomatoes, coarsely chopped

Fresh basil, finely chopped (approximately 1/4 cup)

2 or 3 sprigs fresh thyme

Kosher salt and freshly ground pepper to taste

Splash of fresh lemon juice or wine vinegar

1. Place a large skillet or Dutch oven over medium heat. Add the olive oil to the pan.

2. When the pan is hot, add the chopped onions and garlic and sauté until the onions have wilted, 3 to 4 minutes.

3. Add the squash, peppers, and eggplant and cook until just tender, approximately 12 minutes, stirring regularly.

4. Reduce the heat to low. Add the tomatoes, basil, and thyme, cover the pan, and cook for an additional 30 minutes, or until all the vegetables are tender. Add salt and pepper to taste. Transfer the ratatouille to a large platter with a lip, splashing it with lemon juice just before serving.

Deconstructed Ratatouille

Although this recipe uses essentially the same ingredients as the traditional ratatouille opposite, the end results are very different. By grilling the vegetables and then arranging them separately on a large platter, each person is free to choose their favorites and leave the rest behind. It is a very impressive presentation—colorful glories from the summer garden.

1. Prepare a charcoal or gas-fired grill. Grill the vegetables in batches over medium coals or medium heat on a gas grill, one type of vegetable at a time. Cook just until al dente. Remove from the grill, place on a large platter (keep each vegetable separate), and cover with foil; the vegetables will continue to steam on their own in the covered dish.

2. Arrange the vegetables separately on a big platter, splash them lightly with the oil and vinegar, and sprinkle them with salt and pepper, along with the chopped fresh basil and thyme. Serve with Mediterranean Sauce on the side.

1 large eggplant, trimmed and sliced into ⅜-inch-thick rounds

Green, red, and yellow bell peppers, as many as you like, seeded and quartered

3 to 4 young zucchinis, cut lengthwise into ⅜-inch-thick slices

4 yellow summer squash, split and then halved again if they are big enough

Extra-virgin olive oil

Vinegar or fresh lemon juice

Kosher salt and freshly ground pepper to taste

Fresh basil, finely chopped (approximately ¼ cup)

2 or 3 sprigs fresh thyme

1 recipe Mediterranean Sauce (recipe follows)

Mediterranean Sauce

Combine the mustard and vinegar in a small bowl. Slowly whisk in the olive oil until emulsified. Add the capers and olives and season with pepper.

2 tablespoons Dijon mustard

¼ cup red wine vinegar

¾ cup olive oil

¼ cup capers

¾ cup oil-cured olives, pitted and sliced

Freshly ground pepper to taste

All-American Barbecue

Every summer has a few of those days—the days when you can give yourself up to the grill. From the wafting aroma, the whole neighborhood will know you're cooking ribs, brisket, or maybe even both. Before you know it, the potato salad is made, the ribs are resting, and the backyard is full of something every cook needs: good eaters.

§ New Potato Salad with Grapes and Almonds

§ Brookville Hotel–Style Coleslaw

§ Island Coleslaw

§ No-Fail Barbecue Beef Brisket with Spicy Chili Rub

§ Best-Ever Barbecue Ribs

§ The Mother of All Chocolate Chip Cookies (page 173)

Wine Tip: This menu, which so exemplifies our idea of American cuisine, should have that "American" wine, Zinfandel. (Its origins were probably Eastern European, but it came of age on the West Coast of America.) Consider one of the lush old vine Zinfandels. Oh, some lemonade and a cooler filled with long-neck beers would come in handy too.

New Potato Salad with Grapes and Almonds

America has such an abundance of good potatoes these days that you can change the taste and texture of this salad just by switching from a red B-sized potato to a Yukon Gold or a Yellow Finn.

3 pounds small new potatoes, skins left on

1 pound white grapes, halved, plus additional whole grapes for garnish

1 can (8 ounces) sliced water chestnuts, drained and chopped

4 stalks celery, sliced thin

1 cup lightly toasted slivered almonds (see Note, page 50)

¼ cup chopped fresh dill, or 1 teaspoon dried dill, plus fresh dill for garnish

1½ teaspoons kosher salt

1 teaspoon ground white pepper

1½ cups each of mayonnaise and sour cream, or more if needed

1. Cover the potatoes with water by 4 inches. Bring to a boil, reduce the heat to medium-low, and simmer until the potatoes are tender when pricked with a fork, about 20 minutes. Drain and quarter them.

2. In a large mixing bowl, combine the potatoes, grapes, water chestnuts, celery, almonds, dill, and salt and pepper.

3. Stir in the mayonnaise and sour cream together, and then toss them thoroughly with the salad. You may need more mayonnaise and sour cream, depending on the water content of the potatoes. Add an additional ¼ cup of each until the potatoes and other ingredients are thoroughly coated with the dressing.

4. Cover and chill for 2 hours or overnight. Serve on a big platter with a lip, garnished with grapes and a sprinkling of fresh dill.

Brookville Hotel–Style Coleslaw

Brookville Hotel is a popular restaurant in Abilene, Kansas, that serves fried chicken and all the fixins'. This is our approximation of their delicious coleslaw. We asked the server about it and she shared the secret of layering the dressing ingredients with us.

1. Grate the cabbage. Pour the vinegar over the cabbage, then sprinkle the cabbage with the sugar and the salt. Add the cream.

2. Let the cabbage sit for 20 to 30 minutes without combining all these dressing ingredients, then toss the cabbage, coating it with the dressing. Chill for 2 to 6 hours before serving. The coleslaw will keep for up to 2 days, refrigerated.

1 large head green cabbage

1 cup white vinegar

2/3 cup sugar

1 teaspoon kosher salt

1 cup heavy cream

Island Coleslaw

Serve this sweet-hot coleslaw instead of the Brookville Hotel–Style Coleslaw, or make both and let your guests choose their favorite.

1. In a large bowl, toss together the cabbage, carrots, peanuts, and raisins.

2. In another bowl, combine all the remaining ingredients. Mix to form a dressing, pour it over the cabbage mixture, and toss well. Cover the bowl with plastic wrap and refrigerate for at least one hour.

Note: This coleslaw can be made the night before serving. Simply omit the peanuts and add them to the coleslaw just before serving.

1 medium head green cabbage, finely shredded

2 medium carrots, shredded

3/4 cup salted peanuts

3/4 cup golden raisins

3/4 cup mayonnaise

2 tablespoons granulated sugar

1 tablespoon sesame oil

1 teaspoon kosher salt

3 tablespoons rice wine vinegar

1 teaspoon hot sauce of your choice

1/2 teaspoon ground allspice

1/2 teaspoon ground white pepper

No-Fail Barbecue Beef Brisket with Spicy Chili Rub

The main reason it's so hard to cook brisket is that it starts out as a very tough cut of meat. It's also big, sometimes upward of 13 pounds. We've learned that slow cooking (traditionally for as many as 12 hours) and low cooking (250 degrees is the norm) will tenderize the meat, but such a lengthy process is simply out of the question for most home cooks. After a lot of head-scratching and experimenting, we decided to try a combination of time on the barbecue and time in the oven. Much to our delight, it worked perfectly—approximately 2½ hours on the smoky grill and 3½ hours in the oven, and voilà! Tender, tasty brisket every time. We're aware that 6 hours may still sound like quite a time commitment to some cooks, but the beauty of this method is that, except for the transfer from barbecue to oven, the meat can be left unattended for the entire time.

Don't worry if your brisket is a little larger or smaller than average; split-second cooking times are not critical, since the meat is served very well done. Hickory or mesquite gives the meat its smoky, barbecued flavor, but don't be tempted to overdo a good thing: one packet of smoking wood is all you need. This recipe serves 18 to 24, but barbecuing brisket for less than a crowd is easy to do. Simply ask your butcher for either the "point" (fattier) or "flat" portion (leaner and a little tougher), whichever cut you prefer. Then follow the master recipe, reducing the spice rub by half, the time smoking on the grill to 1½ hours, and the time in the oven to 2 hours.

Moistening the sliced brisket with the meat juices adds flavor, and mixing the juices in equal proportion with good barbecue sauce improves it even further. Serve the brisket with traditional barbecue side dishes such as potato salad or French fries, soft white bread or cornbread, baked beans, coleslaw, dill pickle chips, or greens. Or for a real treat, do like we do in Kansas City: put a couple of slices of brisket on a single piece of regular white bread, add a little coleslaw, several dill pickle chips, and a squirt or two of your favorite barbecue sauce, then fold the whole thing into a neat triangle shape. Good eating!

---

1 recipe Spicy Chili Rub (recipe follows)

1 whole beef brisket (9 to 11 pounds), trimmed

½ bottle (6 ounces) beer

1 bottle (18 ounces) barbecue sauce

1. Apply the spice rub liberally to all sides of the brisket. Wrap it tightly in plastic wrap and refrigerate overnight.

2. One hour prior to cooking, remove the brisket from the refrigerator and unwrap it. Ignite about 3 pounds of charcoal briquettes in a pile on one side of the grill; burn them until they're completely covered with a thin coating of light gray ash, 20 to 30 minutes.

3. Meanwhile, assemble a hickory-chip pouch by wrapping 4 to 6 wood chunks (about 3 inches each) or 3 cups wood chips in a double sheet of heavy-duty foil. Prick at least 6 holes in the top of the foil pouch with a knife tip to allow smoke to escape and place on top of the ash-covered coals.

4. Set the grill rack in place and position the brisket, fat side up, on the side of the rack opposite the fire. Make sure that both top and bottom grill vents are open; position holes in the lid directly over the brisket and cover the grill. Grill-smoke the brisket without removing the lid so that the smoke flavor permeates the meat, approximately 2½ hours.

5. Twenty minutes before the grilling step is done, adjust the oven rack to the middle position and preheat the oven to 300°F. Place the smoked brisket in a baking pan (one with sides) large enough to hold the meat flat. Pour the beer over the brisket and cover the pan tightly with heavy-duty foil. Bake until fork-tender, or until an instant-read thermometer inserted into the thickest portion of meat registers 210°F, 3 to 3½ hours.

6. Remove the brisket from the oven, loosen the foil at one end to release steam, and let it rest for 30 minutes. Drain the juices into a large bowl. Skim and discard the fat from the juices (you should have 1½ to 2 cups liquid left) and mix in equal parts barbecue sauce.

7. Unwrap the brisket and place it on a cutting board. Separate it into two sections. Slice each section on the bias across the grain into thin slices. Moisten the slices with some of the barbecue sauce mixture and serve, passing the remaining sauce separately.

Spicy Chili Rub

Adjust the ingredient amounts or add or subtract ingredients as you wish. For instance, if you cannot abide spicy hot food, reduce or eliminate the cayenne.

Mix all the ingredients together in a jar with a tight-fitting lid. Store any leftovers in the refrigerator or freezer.

¼ **cup paprika**

2 tablespoons each of chili powder, ground cumin, dark brown sugar, and kosher salt

1 tablespoon each of ground oregano, sugar, ground black pepper, and ground white pepper

2 teaspoons cayenne pepper

Best-Ever Barbecue Ribs

If you ever wondered whether or not it was possible to produce "authentic" ribs (the kind you get at a barbecue joint) at home, we're here to tell you the answer—a resounding yes! The following procedure took several years to perfect. We're confident that by following it closely, you'll become the neighborhood barbecue pit master, even if you don't have a pit.

There are three secrets to success with this method: 1) applying the dry rub to the ribs the night before cooking them, 2) cooking them in a covered barbecue using the indirect method, and 3) wrapping the ribs in foil and letting them rest in a paper bag after they've cooked. It sounds a little wacky, we know, but it works. Count on about 4 hours, from start to finish, for this process. This recipe serves 8.

---

4 slabs of pork spareribs (about 12 pounds total)

1 recipe Spicy Chili Rub (page 147), or your favorite store-bought or homemade dry rub

1 recipe Homemade Barbecue Sauce (recipe follows), or your favorite store-bought or homemade barbecue sauce

A kettle grill, or other covered grill

About 3 pounds premium-quality charcoal briquettes (you can use lump natural charcoal, although it may affect cooking times slightly)

Hickory smoking chips (use other types if you prefer)

A rib rack (one that holds the ribs vertically, sideways)

Extra-wide, heavy-duty aluminum foil

2 large brown paper bags, doubled

1. First, pick your ribs. There's not much disagreement here: aficionados from all quarters seem to agree it's the old-fashioned spareribs you want—not baby back ribs, not country-style ribs, just the plain old, under 3 pounds pork spareribs, in one big slab. (When we brought up the fact that other types of ribs were meatier, one knowledgeable friend quickly said, "But I don't want my ribs meaty.") If there is a large amount of extraneous fat on the ribs, trim it before cooking. The amount of fat trimmed from ribs varies, somewhat mysteriously, from one part of the country to another.

2. The night before you intend to grill the ribs, concoct the dry rub and rub a generous amount (about 3 tablespoons) on each side of the ribs. Wrap them tightly in plastic wrap and refrigerate overnight.

3. Start with a grill that's free of any leftover ashes or coals. Light the charcoal briquettes (if you're using one of those metal chimney starters, fill it full). Push all the coals to one side of the fire grate and arrange them in a mound two or three briquettes high. Keep the bottom vents of the grill completely open. The coals are ready when they are covered in a light gray ash. Meanwhile, wrap two large handfuls (about two cups) of hickory smoking chips in foil. Poke small holes in the top of the foil packet with a fork. Contrary to popular practice, there's no real benefit to soaking the chips first. Note: Some folks swear by having a source of moisture inside the grill, most often an aluminum pan of water shoved up next to the coals. As much as this sounds like a good idea and seems to make culinary sense, we were unable to discern any difference each time we tried it. But since it doesn't hurt, feel free to employ it, if desired.

4. Once the coals are ready, lay the foil-wrapped smoking chips on top of the charcoal. Put the cooking grate in place. Position the ribs in the rib rack on the cooking grate opposite the fire. Put the lid on the grill, with the top vents two-thirds of the way open, directly over the ribs. This will help draw the heat and hickory smoke past the ribs. Initially, the heat inside the grill will probably hover around 350°F. Over the approximately 2½-hour cooking period, it will drop a hundred degrees or so—all of which falls into the acceptable slow-cooking range. There is no need to baste the ribs with anything. In all but the most extreme weather conditions, the ribs will be done just about the time the coals burn out.

5. Now for the wacky part: Immediately after taking the ribs off the grill, tightly wrap each slab in heavy-duty aluminum foil. Put the foil-wrapped ribs in a doubled brown paper sack, and fold the sack over the ribs. Allow the ribs to rest at room temperature for 1 hour or more. Although it's difficult to say exactly what happens inside that well-wrapped package, whatever it is, it is good.

6. Finally, heat up 2½ cups of your favorite homemade or store-bought barbecue sauce, unwrap the slabs, swab on the sauce, chop into individual ribs, and then chomp. You may find yourself agreeing with a couple of our friends in Kansas City who had the temerity to suggest, "These ribs are so good, they don't need no sauce!"

Homemade Barbecue Sauce

Heat the butter in a medium saucepan over medium-high heat. Add the onion and garlic; sauté until the onion softens, 3 to 4 minutes. Stir in the lemon juice, pepper, paprika, mustard, hot sauce, and salt; cook over medium heat to blend the flavors, about 5 minutes. Add the vinegar and tomato sauce and bring to a simmer. Simmer uncovered until the sauce thickens slightly, about 15 minutes. Store any leftovers in the refrigerator.

¼ cup (½ stick) butter

1 small onion, peeled and chopped

2 cloves garlic, peeled and minced

2 tablespoons lemon juice

1 tablespoon ground pepper

1 teaspoon each of paprika and dried mustard

½ teaspoon hot sauce

½ teaspoon kosher salt

¼ cup cider vinegar

1 can (16 ounces) tomato sauce

BLT Salad

Summer is the time we want to eat as much fresh corn and tomatoes as possible. It's also the time for BLT sandwiches piled high and that's where we got the inspiration for this entree salad. You have to use your hands to eat the corn "cob-ettes"—that's the fun of it.

1. To make the dressing, put the shallot, paprika, mustard, and vinegar in a blender or food processor. Turn it on and drizzle the oil into the blender. You can make the dressing several hours before you need it.

2. Combine the lettuce, tomatoes, crumbled bacon, corn, and blue cheese. Toss the salad with the dressing and serve.

FOR THE SALAD

2 heads romaine lettuce, washed, drained, and chopped

10 Roma tomatoes or 6 home-grown tomatoes, chopped or quartered

1/2 pound bacon, cooked, drained, and crumbled into bite-sized bits

3 ears corn, blanched and cut into 1-inch pieces

1/2 pound good blue cheese (preferably Maytag blue or Gorgonzola), crumbled

FOR THE DRESSING

1 shallot, peeled and roughly chopped

1/4 cup paprika, either hot or sweet, or a combination

1 tablespoon Dijon mustard

1/2 cup red wine vinegar

1 cup extra-virgin olive oil

Feijoada à la Calistoga

This is the national dish of Brazil, which we suspect is to Brazilians what cassoulet is to the French. Seemingly each and every region of the country has a passion for their particular version and the majority of the country eats it on the same day, at the same time, namely Saturday lunch. What if, instead of running around doing errands, taking kids to soccer games, and getting ready for a dinner party Saturday night, you entertained with a lunch? Alternatively, try making feijoada for a late Sunday lunch.

Feijoada is a melting-pot dish, perfect for America, so please feel free to add something new to the pot—a duck, some organ meats, or perhaps lamb. However, most agree on the side dishes that make the meal complete: rice, collard greens, a vinaigrette, orange slices, and a manioc meal mixture sautéed with egg and butter. Manioc is a large tuber used as a potato in Central and South America.

---

2 pounds dried black beans

1 pound salt pork

3 tablespoons canola oil

1 large onion, peeled and diced

6 cloves garlic, peeled and minced

1 smoked ham hock or shank

2 pounds country-style pork spareribs

2 pounds corned beef, with most but not all of the spices rubbed off

3 bay leaves

1 pound linguica (Portuguese smoked sausage) or Polish or other smoked sausage, cut into 2-inch pieces

Kosher salt and freshly ground pepper to taste

FOR SERVING
3 cups basmati or jasmine rice, cooked according to package directions

1 recipe Collard Greens (recipe follows)

1 recipe Manioc and Eggs (recipe follows)

1 recipe Vinaigrette (page 154)

6 oranges, peeled, halved, and sliced

1. In a large stockpot, cover the black beans with warm water and soak them for at least 2 hours. (Be sure to go through the beans first and pick out any rocks that might be hiding there.)

2. In a medium saucepan, cover the salt pork with cold water and bring it to a boil. Boil for 5 minutes and drain. Cut into bite-sized chunks.

3. In a large Dutch oven or very heavy, large saucepan, heat the canola oil over medium heat. Add the salt pork, onion, and garlic, and sauté until the onions turn translucent, about 7 minutes.

4. Once the beans have finished soaking, drain and return them to the pot. Add enough water to cover the beans by 2 inches. Add the salt pork, garlic, and onion mixture. Bring the pot to a boil, then reduce to a simmer. Cook for 20 minutes, skimming the foam off the top occasionally.

5. Add the ham hock, spareribs, corned beef, and bay leaf to the pot, and simmer for 1 hour. Continue skimming the foam off the top every so often. Add the linguica. When the beans are tender (which could be another hour), season with salt and pepper.

6. Remove the ham hock, ribs, and the corned beef; reserve. Discard the bay leaves. Let the meats rest for 10 or 15 minutes so they don't burn your fingers. Cut the corned beef into bite-sized pieces and return them to the bean pot. Pull or cut the ham and rib meat off the bones and return the meat to the beans, as well.

7. There are six parts to this delicious meal. We don't know what they do in Brazil, but we provide everyone with a pasta bowl with a wide rim. Fill the table with big platters heaped with all the ingredients, separate of course. Each bowl receives some rice, greens, then the feijoada. Finally, sprinkle some of the manioc meal on the feijoada and top with the vinaigrette and orange slices.

Collard Greens

Heat the oil in a large sauté pan over medium heat. Add the garlic and then the greens. Reduce the heat to low and simmer, uncovered, until the greens are tender, about 20 minutes. Add the salt and pepper, to taste. Although greens generally contain plenty of water, if you need to add moisture, add a little chicken broth or apple juice.

2 tablespoons canola oil

3 cloves garlic, peeled and minced

2 bunches collard greens, washed, drained, and chopped

1 teaspoon kosher salt

Ground white pepper to taste

Chicken broth or apple juice, if needed

Manioc and Eggs

Melt the butter in a large sauté pan over low heat. Add the onion and sauté until soft and slightly browned, about 8 to 10 minutes. Add the eggs and scramble them until done. Separate the scrambled eggs into small pieces. Add the manioc meal, parsley, salt, and pepper and cook, stirring well, until lightly browned.

2 tablespoons butter

1 small yellow onion, peeled and finely chopped

2 eggs

2 cups manioc meal, available in Latin grocery stores

1/4 cup chopped fresh parsley leaves

1/2 teaspoon each of kosher salt and freshly ground pepper

Vinaigrette

½ cup olive oil

1 cup red wine vinegar

1 teaspoon kosher salt

1 bunch Italian (flat-leaf) parsley, leaves removed and finely chopped

4 tomatoes, chopped

1 yellow onion, peeled and chopped

2 fresh jalapeño peppers, seeded and diced

Combine all the ingredients in a glass jar with a tight-fitting lid. Let sit for at least an hour before serving. Don't make it the night before, however, as the parsley loses its color and flavor after several hours. Shake the jar to remix the dressing right before serving.

Wine Tip: Brazil isn't known for its wine-growing regions, so after you have a caipirinha, those delicious cocktails that Brazil is known for (they're made with cachaça, a distilled sugarcane liquor), travel to Argentina for a bottle of Malbec or to Chile for a Carmenere. They're in the neighborhood.

Lulu's Lamb Ribs

Denver-style ribs are lamb riblets, parts of the lamb breast that are trimmed of fat and connective tissue, about 3 to 5 inches long. Ask your butcher to order them a few days ahead.

4 to 5 pounds Denver-style lamb ribs

FOR THE MARINADE

1 cup sherry

¾ cup sesame oil

Juice of 3 limes

6 tablespoons hot sauce

1 cup creamy peanut butter

1. Cut the ribs into serving pieces. In a mixing bowl, combine the marinade ingredients. Put the ribs in large Ziploc bags and divide the marinade between the bags. Close the bags and make sure the ribs are coated with the marinade. Refrigerate for at least 4 hours.

2. Remove the ribs from the refrigerator approximately 20 minutes before grilling.

3. Prepare a charcoal or gas-fired grill. Grill the ribs directly over a moderately hot fire. (Because of the sherry and peanut butter in the marinade, the chops will have a tendency to blacken if cooked over too hot a fire.) Turn them every 3 minutes or so; depending on their thickness, they will cook in 8 to 12 minutes. Once cooked, remove them from the grill and serve on a large platter.

Wine Tip: We're going to go against the usual "red wine with red meat" here and opt for white wine for these tasty little morsels. We vote for a high-acidity wine that should cut right through all the char and richness. In a word, Riesling.

Summer Street Food Party

The informality of food you can eat with your hands makes for a fun, decidedly casual meal, perfect for the long days and warm nights of summer. The following three recipes—a United Nations approach to a menu if there ever was one—have something for everyone, young, old, and in between.

§ **Lamb Burgers with Mint Yogurt Dressing**

§ **Fish Tacos with Mexican Cabbage Salad**

§ **Iowa Corn Dogs**

§ **Lulu's Panzanella (page 42)**

§ **Three Melon Salad (page 162)**

§ **Black-Bottom Cupcakes (page 177)**

Wine Tip: Because you're serving casual food, both red meat and white fish, and we won't even think about matching the hot dogs, make a big pitcher of ice tea, chill some bottles of Beaujolais slightly, and open up a nice bottle of Pinot Grigio.

Lamb Burgers with Mint Yogurt Dressing

We're betting that even people who claim not to like lamb will like this variation on a favorite street food, known as *kefta,* from Morocco and Lebanon. A traditional kefta is spiraled around a skewer and looks more like a sausage than a patty. Our burgers are easier to handle on the grill; just make sure they will fit in the pita pockets.

1. In a small bowl, combine the yogurt, chopped mint, and salt. Set aside.

2. Combine the lamb, dill, red pepper flakes, garlic, and salt and pepper. Divide the ground meat mixture into 8 portions and form each into an oval shape that will fit into a pocket pita. Lightly brush a grill pan with vegetable oil and place it over medium heat. When the pan is hot but not smoking, place the patties on the pan and cook for 3 minutes per side for a medium-rare burger.

3. Use a knife or scissors to cut off the top part of each pita to form an opening; put the cut part in the bottom of the pita to keep it from getting too soggy. Serve the burgers in the pocket pitas topped with the yogurt dressing.

FOR THE BURGERS

2 pounds ground lamb

1 teaspoon dried dill

$1/2$ teaspoon crushed red pepper flakes

4 cloves garlic, pushed through a garlic press

2 teaspoons kosher salt

Freshly ground pepper to taste

Vegetable oil, for the grill pan

Pocket pitas

FOR THE YOGURT DRESSING

2 cups plain yogurt

$1/4$ cup chopped fresh mint

$1/2$ teaspoon kosher salt

Fish Tacos with Mexican Cabbage Salad

The past few years have seen the steady migration of fish tacos across the country—simply because they are so good. The combination of flavors is a satisfying one, and they're light enough that you can eat more than one without feeling gordo (fat!). Although many taquerias and Mexican restaurants bread and deep-fry the fish, we much prefer marinating and then grilling it. Some taquerias serve lettuce in their fish tacos, but we've found this salad to be a much more satisfying accompaniment.

---

2 pounds mild white fish fillets, such as red snapper or catfish, cut into 1-inch-wide strips

12 bamboo skewers

FOR THE MARINADE

¼ cup light vegetable oil, such as canola

Juice of 2 limes and 1 lemon

1 teaspoon each of crumbled dried oregano leaves, ground cumin, kosher salt, and freshly ground pepper

ACCOMPANIMENTS

8 corn tortillas

1 recipe Mexican Cabbage Salad (recipe follows)

1 or 2 avocados, cut into thin slices

2 tomatoes, cut into thin wedges

Chopped fresh cilantro

Lime wedges

Your favorite hot sauce

1. Combine the marinade ingredients in a small bowl and mix well. Place the strips of fish in the marinade and set aside at room temperature for 20 to 30 minutes. Don't leave the fish in the marinade any longer, or the acid in the citrus juices will "cook" the fish.

2. Prepare a hot charcoal or gas-fired grill. Thread the fish strips onto the skewers, accordion style. Position the skewered fish directly over the coals. Cook 4 to 5 minutes per side, turning once. The fish is done when it is uniformly white all the way through. While the fish cooks, wrap the tortillas in foil and place them on the grill next to the fish. They will be soft and warm by the time the fish is done.

3. To serve, place a couple of pieces of fish in each tortilla along with a little of the salad, some avocado and tomato slices, chopped cilantro, a squeeze of lime, and a little of your favorite hot sauce. Serve immediately.

Mexican Cabbage Salad

Combine all the ingredients in a large bowl and mix well. Cover and refrigerate the salad until serving time.

4 cups grated green cabbage (about 1 small cabbage)

1 apple, peeled and grated

1 small onion, finely minced

1/2 cup mayonnaise

2 tablespoons fresh lemon juice

1 teaspoon ground cumin

Kosher salt and freshly ground pepper

Iowa Corn Dogs

A couple of summers ago we were in charge of the corn dog station at a neighborhood backyard barbecue. At least we got to talk to everyone at the party, because sooner or later they were all lined up at our table. No matter what else is on the menu, count on everyone wanting at least one corn dog. This recipe is from the Iowa State Fair—the real McCoy. It originally appeared in *Saveur* magazine.

1. Sift together the flour, cornmeal, sugar, baking powder, and mustard into a bowl. Whisk together the egg, milk, and 2 teaspoons oil in another bowl. Add the milk mixture to the flour mixture, beating with a wooden spoon until the batter is smooth.

2. Pour vegetable oil into a large, heavy pot to a depth of 3 inches. Over medium heat, heat the oil to 350°F. Meanwhile, dry the hot dogs with paper towels, then place them on the wooden skewers. Dip the hot dogs into the batter until evenly coated. Gently place the coated hot dogs in the hot oil and fry them, turning once or twice, until crisp and golden, 3 to 4 minutes. Drain on paper towels. Serve with mustard and ketchup for dipping, if you like.

1 cup flour

2/3 cup yellow cornmeal

2 tablespoons sugar

1 1/2 teaspoons baking powder

1/4 teaspoon dried mustard

1 egg, lightly beaten

3/4 cup milk

2 teaspoons vegetable oil, plus more for frying

8 hot dogs

8 wooden skewers

Curried Chicken Salad

Some things are just meant to go together; fruit and chicken are two of those things.

1. Rinse the chicken breasts, place them in a large stockpot, and cover them with cold water. Add the onion and celery (bottoms and tops). Bring to a boil and simmer until the chicken is tender and cooked, approximately 45 minutes. Remove the breasts from the stock and cool. Once cool, remove the chicken meat from the bones and chop it into bite-sized pieces.

2. In a large bowl, combine the chicken, cashews, grapes, sliced celery, and pineapple.

3. Combine the dressing ingredients in a separate bowl. Toss the salad with the dressing and chill for at least 2 hours or overnight. To serve, transfer the chicken salad to a big platter.

Wine Tip: The melon and grapefruit aromas and flavors of a New Zealand Sauvignon Blanc are lovely with this dish. Although Lulu started her love affair with New Zealand Sauvignon Blanc with Cloudy Bay, she's learned that there are loads of good wines from that country. Lately we've enjoyed drinking Kim Crawford from the Marlborough region of New Zealand, which has a screw-off top.

5 pounds bone-in chicken breasts

1 small onion, peeled and quartered

Bottom and tops of a few heads of celery, coarsely chopped

1 cup cashews, roughly chopped

1 pound white grapes, halved

4 to 6 stalks celery, sliced

1 medium-sized ripe pineapple, peeled and diced

FOR THE CURRY DRESSING

1 tablespoon curry powder

2 teaspoons Dijon mustard

1/2 teaspoon ground cardamom

1 cup each of mayonnaise and sour cream

1/2 cup plain yogurt

Juice of 1 lime

1/2 teaspoon kosher salt

Scallops and Corn

Fresh corn and scallops are a great seasonal taste combination, one that just isn't the same in the dead of winter with south-of-the-border corn.

1½ to 2 pounds sea scallops, rinsed and patted dry

1 cup sriracha chili-garlic sauce

½ cup soy sauce

⅓ cup rice wine vinegar

¼ cup sesame oil

½ cup (1 stick) butter

4 shallots, peeled and sliced

3 red, yellow, or green bell peppers, or a combination, seeded, quartered, and diced

8 ears corn, kernels cut off the cob

1 can (14 ounces) coconut milk

½ cup half-and-half

1 teaspoon kosher salt

½ teaspoon freshly ground pepper

2 cups cherry tomatoes, halved

⅓ cup chopped fresh basil

1. Combine the scallops, hot sauce, soy sauce, vinegar, and sesame oil in a large storage container or Ziploc bag. Marinate for at least an hour but not more than 3 hours or the vinegar will "cook" the seafood.

2. Melt the butter in a large sauté pan over low heat. Add the shallots and bell peppers and sauté for 5 minutes, then add the corn kernels. Sauté over low heat until the peppers are tender, another 5 minutes. Add the coconut milk, half-and-half, and salt and pepper and cook another 5 minutes. Add the cherry tomatoes and heat through, 2 to 3 minutes. Remove from the heat but cover to keep warm.

3. Heat a large, dry sauté pan over medium heat. Sear the marinated scallops 3 to 4 minutes on each side, being careful not to crowd them. The marinade clinging to the scallops should be sufficient moisture for cooking them, but you can always add a tablespoon or two of the marinade when necessary.

4. If you have marinade left when all the scallops are cooked, pour it into the sauté pan and simmer it for 5 minutes, then drizzle the cooked scallops with the sauce.

5. When both the corn and the scallops are ready, turn the corn and cherry tomatoes onto a large platter with a lip. Place the scallops on top and garnish with the chopped basil.

Wine Tip: This dish is a pairing that is only missing one thing: the Chardonnay to drink with it. I wouldn't splurge on a white Burgundy but a good Australian or Californian Chardonnay would be great.

Swiss Chard and Goat Cheese Tart

This savory tart—a combination of eggs, cheese, and greens—is a great summer brunch dish. Vegetarians in the crowd will particularly appreciate it.

1. Heat the oil over medium heat in a large sauté pan. Add the onion and sauté until soft, about 7 minutes. Add the chopped chard and cook until wilted, 15 to 20 minutes. Add the raisins and remove from the heat.

2. In a mixing bowl, beat the eggs. Add the Parmesan.

3. Line the tart pan with the crust dough. Crumble the goat cheese, spreading it over the crust. Then add the chard mixture to the pan, spreading it evenly. Pour the egg and cheese mixture on top. Bake at 350°F for approximately 40 minutes, or until the top of the tart is browned and the middle is set.

Wine Tip: Goat cheese and Sancerre are it.

3 tablespoons olive oil

1 onion, peeled and diced

2 bunches Swiss chard, washed, drained, and chopped

½ cup golden raisins

4 eggs

½ cup freshly grated Parmesan cheese

1 recipe Pie Crust (recipe follows), or a store-bought 10-inch pie crust

4 ounces goat cheese

Pie Crust

1. Put the flour and salt in the bowl of a food processor. Add the butter, a few pieces at a time, pulsing between each addition.

2. Remove any ice cubes from the water and slowly drizzle the water into the flour and butter mixture, pulsing just until the dough forms a ball. You may not need all the water.

3. Flatten the ball into a disk, wrap the dough in plastic, and chill for at least an hour.

4. This recipe makes two 10-inch crusts or a two-crust pie. You can make the dough the night before you need it, and then let it sit at room temperature for 30 minutes before rolling it out.

4 cups all-purpose flour

1 teaspoon kosher salt

1 cup (2 sticks) butter, cut into 1-inch pieces

1 cup ice water

Three Melon Salad

These three melons, which used to be relegated to the breakfast table, take on a more sophisticated flavor with the addition of basil, mint, and salty ricotta salata—without diminishing the lusciousness of the melons. This grown-up version of melon salad could accompany almost any summer entree. You can peel and chop your melons 4 to 5 hours before you need them. Just chill them in a Ziploc bag or storage container. Don't assemble the salad more than 3 hours ahead of time, however, even if you plan to chill it first. The vinegar will start to break down the meat of the melon.

---

9 cups melon chunks, equal parts cantaloupe, honeydew, and watermelon

1 teaspoon kosher salt

15 to 20 basil leaves, chopped

12 to 15 mint leaves

1 cup extra-virgin olive oil

⅓ cup sherry vinegar

¼ pound ricotta salata, shaved into thin pieces

In a large bowl, combine the melon, salt, basil, mint, oil, and vinegar together, tossing to distribute the ingredients. Sprinkle with the cheese. Let stand at room temperature for at least 30 minutes before serving.

Figs, Nectarines, and Prosciutto

Even in this day and age of instant gratification, when everything edible is available all the time, fresh figs remain a special treat, available only a couple of times a year, in the spring and late summer. This dish creates a "fig memory" that will help you remember how great they taste the other ten months of the year.

1. To prepare the dressing, combine the wine, water, and sugar in a saucepan and bring to a boil. Lower the heat to medium and reduce until the mixture resembles runny syrup. Add the vinegar and cook 3 minutes more. Remove from the heat and allow to cool to room temperature. You can make the dressing ahead of time and refrigerate it if you'd like.

2. Arrange the figs and nectarines on a platter. Top with the strips of prosciutto and drizzle all over with the dressing.

1 cup each of white wine and water

1 cup sugar

1/3 cup balsamic vinegar

2 pints fresh figs, halved or quartered, depending on the size

6 to 8 ripe nectarines, pitted and sliced

1/2 pound prosciutto, thinly sliced into strips

Salade Niçoise with Swordfish and Black Rice

This is a variation of the classic salade niçoise from the Riviera. Replacing the more customary canned tuna is grilled swordfish, along with the rather exotic black rice (purported to have once been grown exclusively for the Chinese emperor's use), which has a nutty taste and soft texture. This is a beautiful salad, hearty enough to serve as main course with some warm, crusty French bread and a well-chilled dry white wine. Because this is a room temperature meal, you can grill the swordfish ahead of time.

1. Combine the ingredients for the vinaigrette and mix well with a wire whisk. Prepare the black (or brown) rice according to package instructions. Reserve in the refrigerator until needed.

2. Wash the swordfish under cold water; pat dry with paper towels. Brush with olive oil and sprinkle lightly with salt and pepper to taste.

3. Prepare a charcoal or gas grill. Grill the swordfish steaks directly over a hot fire for about 5 minutes per side, turning once using a spatula halfway through the cooking process. The swordfish is done when it's still slightly pink at the center; take a peek *(continued)*

5 to 6 fresh swordfish steaks (3 to 3½ pounds total), each 1 inch thick

Olive oil, for brushing the fish

Kosher salt and freshly ground pepper to taste

1 cup black rice, sometimes sold as "Forbidden Rice," or brown rice if unavailable

8 medium-sized new potatoes

1½ pounds green beans, ends and strings removed

8 cups lettuce greens, washed and thoroughly dried

3 large tomatoes, cut into wedges

3 hard-boiled eggs, quartered

½ cup black olives (preferably the small niçoise olive)

2 tablespoons capers

12 anchovy fillets, drained (optional)

FOR THE VINAIGRETTE DRESSING
¾ cup extra-virgin olive oil

¼ cup red wine vinegar

½ teaspoon Dijon mustard

1 tablespoon finely chopped green onions

2 tablespoons finely chopped fresh parsley

⅛ teaspoon kosher salt

Freshly ground pepper to taste

with a sharp knife to be sure. When the fish is done, put it on a plate, loosely tent with aluminum foil, and reserve in the refrigerator until needed.

4. Cook the potatoes in boiling salted water for about 15 minutes, or until the tip of a sharp knife can be inserted easily through the middle of the potatoes. Drain and immediately plunge the potatoes into ice water to stop the cooking process. Drain again and slice into ¼-inch-thick slices. Pour enough of the vinaigrette over the potatoes to coat lightly; reserve in the refrigerator until needed.

5. Cook the green beans in boiling salted water for 7 to 10 minutes, or until just tender. Drain and immediately plunge into ice water to stop the cooking process. Drain again. Reserve in the refrigerator until needed.

6. To assemble the salad, scatter the chilled lettuce greens in an even layer on a large platter. Arrange the rice, potatoes, tomato wedges, hard-boiled eggs, and green beans in mounds evenly spaced around the platter. Break up the grilled swordfish steaks into good-sized chunks and arrange the fish in its own mound. Sprinkle the black olives and capers all over the salad; garnish with anchovy fillets if desired. Pour the remaining dressing over all the ingredients and let your guests help themselves. A delicious warm-weather meal!

Wine Tip: When you make this dish, we're sure you'll imagine yourself on a glamorous yacht in the harbor at Cannes, if just for a minute. What would you drink in the South of France? Ask your wine merchant to show you what white wine he has from the Côtes de Provence, or drink Rosé. Another budget tip: Perrin Réserve wines from the Côtes du Rhône are consistently drinkable, both the white and the red.

Southeast Asian Party by the Pool

What better cuisine for a hot summer night than a menu inspired by the food of Thailand and Vietnam? The satays can be grilled ahead of time and served at room temperature. The peanut noodles and marinated cucumbers can be made in the cool of the morning and held in the refrigerator until dinnertime. Who said it's too hot to cook?

§ **Pork Satay (page 10)**
§ **Cold Asian Noodles with Peanut Sauce**
§ **Marinated Cucumbers**
§ **Viet-Caramelized Chicken Wings**
§ **Peach Crisp (page 172)**

Wine Tip: There are plenty of good Asian beers to pair with this food. But Lulu prefers wine. Try the Portuguese Alvarinho Vinho Verde, or young (green) wine. It's given a small shot of nitrogen to create a little frizzante, and it's just the ticket with all these spicy flavors.

Cold Asian Noodles with Peanut Sauce

If you can find fresh Chinese egg noodles, they are really good in this dish. They are usually kept in the refrigerator case at Asian markets.

1. Prepare the noodles according to the package directions. Toss with the canola oil and refrigerate if you prefer to serve the noodles chilled. Otherwise, they can be served at room temperature.

2. In a large bowl, combine the remaining ingredients except for the garnishes, and mix well. Toss the noodles with this dressing at the last minute. Put the peanut noodles on a big platter, surround them with the marinated cucumbers, and garnish with cilantro, peanuts, and black sesame seeds.

1 pound fresh Chinese egg noodles or angel hair pasta or fettuccine if not available

2 tablespoons canola oil, for the noodles

1/2 cup rice wine vinegar

1/3 cup each of Thai sweet chili sauce or sriracha chili-garlic sauce, sesame oil, and canola oil

1/4 cup medium-bodied soy sauce, such as Pearl River Soy or low-salt Kikkoman brands

Juice of 1 lime

3/4 cup crunchy peanut butter

1-inch piece of fresh ginger, peeled and minced

1 teaspoon kosher salt

Cilantro leaves, salted peanuts, and black sesame seeds, for garnish

1 recipe Marinated Cucumbers (page 168)

Marinated Cucumbers

2 cucumbers, sliced thin

1 white onion, peeled and sliced

1 cup sugar

1 teaspoon kosher salt

1 cup white vinegar

Water to cover

Combine the cucumbers and onion with the sugar, salt, and vinegar in a Ziploc bag or storage container. Cover with water and marinate in the refrigerator for at least 3 hours or overnight.

Viet-Caramelized Chicken Wings

This method of cooking with the caramel sauce is used in Vietnamese cuisine for a variety of meats: chicken, duck, and all kinds of seafood and fish. They are an interesting alternative to the more mundane hot chicken wings that are so popular in America right now.

1 cup sugar

¾ cup nuoc-nam (Vietnamese fish sauce)

2 pounds chicken wings

2- to 4-inch piece of fresh ginger, peeled and thinly sliced

6 cloves garlic, peeled and thinly sliced

2 stalks lemon grass, sliced into 3-inch pieces

2 kaffir lime leaves (available dried or in the freezer section of Asian grocery stores)

4 shallots, thinly sliced

Cilantro leaves, black sesame seeds, or sliced green onions, for garnish

1. To make the caramel sauce, melt the sugar in a heavy saucepan over low heat, stirring constantly. When the sugar is brown, 20 to 25 minutes, remove it from the heat and add the fish sauce. The mixture will bubble up. Put the pan back on the heat until the sugar is completely dissolved, about 5 minutes. Cool before using. The sauce can be made up to a week before using.

2. Rinse the chicken wings and pat them dry with paper towels. Combine all the ingredients except the garnish, including the cooled caramel sauce and the chicken wings, in a heavy sauté pan or Dutch oven. Bring to a boil. Simmer for 30 to 40 minutes, or until the chicken is tender. Stir every 10 minutes or so to get all the wings evenly browned. Arrange the wings on a big platter and garnish them with a sprinkle of cilantro and black sesame seeds.

Chicken Livers with Wilted Spinach

The idea of this entree salad is to sauté the chicken livers, place them on top of the spinach, and then wilt the spinach with the wonderful pan drippings from cooking the livers. We stuck some croutons on the bottom to absorb all the good stuff.

4 cups bread cubes from an Italian or French loaf

⅔ cup olive oil

½ cup canola oil

2 pounds chicken livers

1 cup all-purpose flour seasoned with 1 teaspoon kosher salt, ½ teaspoon freshly ground pepper, and ½ teaspoon paprika

1 pound baby spinach leaves, cleaned and drained

1 cup red wine vinegar

Pinch of kosher salt

1. Preheat the oven to 325°F.

2. In a large mixing bowl, toss the bread cubes with ⅓ cup of the olive oil. Place them on a baking sheet and toast until the outside of the bread is hard to the touch but the inside is still soft, about 10 minutes.

3. In a large sauté pan, heat the canola oil to medium heat. Dredge the livers in the seasoned flour and fry them, turning once, until they are just cooked, 10 to 12 minutes. Be careful—the livers will splatter as they cook in the oil. Drain them on several layers of paper towel. Reserve the juices in the sauté pan.

4. Put a layer of the toasted bread cubes on a big platter and top with the spinach. Place the cooked livers on top of the spinach.

5. Add the vinegar and the remaining ⅓ cup olive oil to the sauté pan in which the livers were cooked. Place over low heat, add the pinch of salt, and let the vinaigrette simmer for 2 minutes or so. Pour it over the livers, spinach, and croutons, and serve immediately.

Wine Tip: The only thing this dish says to us emphatically is "I want red wine." Pick a region of Spain and do some tasting—it will be really satisfying. Rioja? Ribera del Duero? You need a little tannin to cut through the richness of the livers. P. S. After writing this, we made the dish again and drank sherry with it. It was marvelous; either fino or amontillado.

Big Platter Desserts

Big Platter is all about opening your heart and your table to others with a minimum of fuss. Now that you've done such a good job of leaving time for the real joy of hospitality—entertaining your guests—you don't want to finish the meal with a labor-intensive dessert. You want the grand finale to be something that you can put out on the buffet with a big spoon and some plates beside it so guests can help themselves, or a cookie or cupcake that they can grab. Dessert should be a sweet ending for everyone, including the host, not a giant project that leaves you with a sour taste in your mouth.

Peach Crisp

This crisp topping also goes well with Jonathan apples in the fall. Just substitute apples for the peaches and leave out the blueberries.

FOR THE FRUIT

16 ripe peaches (about 6 pounds)

1 tablespoon fresh lemon juice

2 tablespoons sugar

1 tablespoon all-purpose flour

1 cup fresh blueberries

FOR THE TOPPING

½ cup (1 stick) butter

1 cup old-fashioned rolled oats, uncooked

1 cup brown sugar

1⅓ cups all-purpose flour

⅓ cup dark molasses

1. Preheat the oven to 350°F.

2. To prepare the fruit, bring a stockpot full of water to a boil. Make an X with a paring knife through the skin on the end of each peach opposite the stem. Plunge the peaches in the boiling water, then take them out with tongs or a flat strainer and place them in a large bowl of ice water. Once the peaches have cooled, the skins will slip off easily with the help of your paring knife.

3. Slice the peaches into a large, round casserole dish and sprinkle them with the lemon juice. Toss with the sugar and flour and sprinkle with the blueberries.

4. To make the topping, melt the butter over medium heat in a heavy saucepan. Reduce the heat to low and add the oats, brown sugar, flour, and molasses. Stir to combine with the melted butter until a dough-like ball is formed and the pan comes clean as you stir.

5. Turn this sticky dough out on top of the fruit and, with a small spatula or your hands, spread the topping evenly over the fruit. Be careful—the mixture will still be warm. Bring the mixture to the sides of the casserole to seal in the juices during baking.

6. Bake the crisp until browned and bubbly on top, about 50 minutes. This is even better with vanilla ice cream. But you knew that.

The Mother of All Chocolate Chip Cookies

This is basically one big cookie pressed into a large baking sheet. Beyond its size, it's a really good chocolate chip cookie—really good. Hats off to our friend Laura Behrens for sharing this recipe with us.

---

1. Preheat the oven to 350°F.

2. In a large bowl, mix the flour, salt, and baking soda and set aside.

3. By hand or with an electric mixer, cream together the butter, sugar, and brown sugar until smooth.

4. Add the eggs, milk, and vanilla to the butter mixture and blend well. Add the dry ingredients to the wet ingredients and mix well. Fold in the chocolate chips and chopped nuts, if using.

5. Press the dough in an even layer onto an ungreased 12 x 16-inch cookie sheet. Bake the cookie, checking for doneness after 25 minutes. The cookie should be golden brown on top. Depending on how well-done you like your chocolate chip cookies (and whether or not you like crunchy corners and edges), the baking time may double.

6. Remove the cookie from the oven, let it cool, and cut into squares.

6 cups all-purpose flour

3 teaspoons kosher salt

1 teaspoon baking soda

2½ cups (5 sticks) butter, at room temperature

2 cups sugar

1 cup each of light and dark brown sugar

2 eggs

5 tablespoons milk

2 tablespoons vanilla extract

1 cup each of semisweet chocolate chips and white chocolate chips

2 cups chopped pecans or walnuts, or a combination (optional)

Plum Clafouti

Maybe a name change would increase this delicious dessert's reputation. . . . We can't figure out why more people aren't familiar with it. Traditionally made with cherries, clafouti originated in the Limousin region of south-central France. Making it is simplicity itself, and the results are satisfying in that homey, comforting way. Make it once, and we guarantee you'll make it again. Feel free to substitute cherries, pears, apples, or berries for the plums, if desired. If the fruit is very juicy, you'll need to increase the flour to a full cup, or even slightly more.

1¼ cups milk

⅔ cup sugar

3 large eggs

2 teaspoons vanilla extract

Pinch of kosher salt

½ cup all-purpose flour

3 cups plums, pitted and quartered

1. Preheat the oven to 350°F.

2. Put the milk, sugar, eggs, vanilla, salt, and flour in a food processor and mix until smooth.

3. Liberally butter the bottom of a large pie dish or a 10-inch cast-iron skillet. Spread the plums evenly over the bottom of the dish. Pour the batter over the top of the fruit.

4. Bake until the top is browned and a knife inserted in the middle of the clafouti comes out clean, 45 to 50 minutes.

Sweet Birthday Party

We all love hosting a birthday party for someone special in our lives. A dessert buffet gives a birthday party definition right away. If the party is for someone younger in your household, a movie, a trip to the skating rink, or a baseball game can be followed up with sweets and presents at home. If the honoree is an older relative or friend, you can have a Sunday afternoon dessert party so everyone gets home before dark.

§ **Flourless Chocolate Torte**

§ **Black-Bottom Cupcakes**

§ **Twisted Trifle of your choice**

§ **Baked Pears with Mascarpone and Amaretti**

§ **Pumpkin Flan with Sweet Tortilla Chips**

Wine Tip: If your guests have reached the legal drinking age, then offer coffee with an assortment of liquors such as brandy, Irish cream liqueur, B & B, or grappa. Or pour little glasses of Vin Santo from Italy or a late harvest wine from California.

Flourless Chocolate Torte

As elegant and rich as this cake is, making it is the essence of simplicity—and it's a wonderful treat for chocoholics. Serve it with a small scoop of good vanilla ice cream or a dollop of whipped cream.

---

12 ounces bittersweet chocolate

3 cups (6 sticks) butter, plus more for pan

12 eggs, separated

1¼ cups sugar, plus more for pan

1. Preheat the oven to 325°F.

2. Melt the chocolate and butter in the top of a double boiler or a stainless-steel mixing bowl placed over a pan of boiling water. Remove from the heat.

3. In a separate bowl, whisk the egg yolks and sugar until smooth.

4. In another bowl, whip the egg whites until they hold soft peaks, about 12 minutes.

5. Blend the egg yolk–sugar mixture into the melted chocolate-butter mixture. Fold the beaten egg whites into the batter.

6. Butter the bottom and sides of a 9-inch springform pan. Dust it lightly with sugar. Pour the batter into the pan and bake for 40 to 45 minutes, or until the cake is cracked on top.

Black-Bottom Cupcakes

We've never met anyone who hasn't fallen for these decadent, devil's food–like cupcakes with creamy, chocolaty centers—in fact, they may be addictive! Adapted for us by Ed Gould from an old *Bon Appétit* magazine, this recipe is a winner. Just one last thing: Got milk?

1. Preheat the oven to 375°F.

2. In a medium bowl, thoroughly mix the cream cheese, eggs, sugar, and salt using a wooden spoon. Fold in the chocolate chips. Set aside until needed.

3. In a large bowl, combine the dry ingredients—the flour, sugar, brown sugar, cocoa, baking soda, and salt.

4. Add the wet ingredients—the water, oil, vinegar, vanilla, and sour cream—to the dry ingredients and blend thoroughly to form a smooth batter.

5. Line three cupcake tins (twelve cupcakes per tin) with paper liners. Fill each about three-quarters full with batter. Drop 1 tablespoon of the cream cheese mixture in the center of each.

6. Bake for approximately 30 minutes. The cupcakes are done when a toothpick inserted into the cake part (not the gooey center) comes out clean. Cool them for 10 to 15 minutes, then remove them from the tins.

FOR THE CREAM CHEESE MIXTURE

2 packages (16 ounces total) cream cheese, at room temperature

2 large eggs

$2/3$ cup sugar

$1/8$ teaspoon kosher salt

1 package (12 ounces) semisweet chocolate chips

FOR THE CHOCOLATE BATTER

3 cups all-purpose flour

1 cup sugar

$1/2$ cup each of dark brown sugar and unsweetened powdered cocoa

2 teaspoons baking soda

$1/8$ teaspoon kosher salt

$1 1/3$ cups water

$2/3$ cup vegetable oil

2 tablespoons white vinegar

1 tablespoon vanilla extract

1 large container (16 ounces) sour cream

Two Twisted Trifles

Both tiramisù and trifle are perfect Big Platter dishes that need only a serving spoon, some dessert plates, and forks or spoons for serving. We wanted to combine the coffee and chocolate flavors of the tiramisù with the traditional trifle form. Our tests resulted in two great versions. Let them chill at least 4 hours but not longer than 24—otherwise the whipped cream will start to separate.

Tiramisù Trifle

16-ounce pound cake, plus a few slices more if needed (frozen, store-bought cake is fine)

3 tablespoons cornstarch

¼ cup instant espresso granules

¾ cup sugar

Dash of kosher salt

2 cups milk

3 ounces semisweet chocolate (at least 50 percent cocoa)

½ cup Godiva liqueur or other chocolate liqueur

1 cup strong coffee, poured in a pie plate or some other flat pan and cooled

1 pint heavy cream

1 teaspoon vanilla extract

Trifle bowl or another glass bowl with straight sides

1. Measure the sides of your bowl and cut ⅓-inch-thick slices of pound cake so that the cake will ring the sides of the bowl and cover the bottom. You will also need a few additional slices for layering when you assemble the dessert.

2. Make a double boiler by filling a stockpot halfway with water and fitting a stainless-steel mixing bowl on the top. Bring the water to a boil.

3. Remove the mixing bowl from the pot. Combine the cornstarch, instant espresso, ½ cup of the sugar, and the salt in the bowl. Add ½ cup of the milk and whisk to form a paste. Put the bowl back over the boiling water.

4. In a saucepan, bring the remaining 1½ cups milk and two-thirds of the chocolate to a boil. Watch carefully so the milk doesn't boil over. When the milk is scalded, add the chocolate milk mixture to the sugar mixture and let it cook on top of the double boiler until it forms a thick pudding, stirring often but not continuously. Remove from the heat and allow it to cool for 10 minutes, still stirring every once in a while so it will not form a skin.

5. Add the chocolate liqueur to the cooled coffee. Dip one side of each slice of pound cake in the coffee-chocolate liqueur mixture and line the sides and bottom of the bowl, placing the dipped side of the cake facing inward.

6. Using an electric beater or a whisk, whip the cream to soft peaks, adding the remaining ¼ cup sugar and the vanilla when the cream starts to thicken. Chop the remaining third of the chocolate.

7. Now you should have four things ready to build your trifle: the cake-lined trifle dish plus some extra slices of pound cake, the chocolate-coffee pudding, the whipped cream, and the chopped chocolate.

8. Spoon a layer of the pudding over the layer of cake in the bottom of the trifle dish. This should take one-third to one-half of the pudding. If your bowl has sloped sides, save more than half of your pudding; the next layer will require more pudding.

9. Spoon on a layer of whipped cream and sprinkle with some of the chopped chocolate. Make another layer of dipped cake slices, then repeat the sequence of pudding, whipped cream, and chopped chocolate. This should get you to the top of the bowl. Cover and chill at least 4 hours before serving.

Butterscotch and Baileys Trifle

This dessert really thrills butterscotch-loving souls such as Lulu. You follow the same procedure as for the first trifle recipe, just change the flavor—the chocolate pudding becomes butterscotch, Baileys instead of Godiva is combined with the coffee for dipping the cake, and the layers are topped with chopped up Heath Bars instead of semisweet chocolate.

1. Prepare the pound cake as in step 1 of the tiramisù trifle. Create a double boiler as in step 2.

2. In the stainless-steel mixing bowl, combine the brown sugar, cornstarch, salt, and ½ cup of the milk to form a paste. In a saucepan, scald the remaining 1½ cups milk and the butter. Combine the scalded milk mixture with the brown sugar mixture and cook until it forms a thick pudding, stirring often. Remove from the heat and cool for 10 minutes.

3. When you're ready to build the trifle, combine the Baileys and the coffee for dipping the cake, and whip the cream with the sugar and vanilla until soft peaks form. Assemble the trifle as described in the tiramisù version, substituting the chopped toffee for the chopped chocolate. If you favor a toffee that is not coated in chocolate, please use that; this dish is rich enough to not miss the added chocolate. Build the trifle as described in steps 8 and 9 of the tiramisù recipe. Cover and chill for at least 4 hours before serving.

16-ounce pound cake

½ cup light brown sugar

3 tablespoons cornstarch

Dash of kosher salt

2 cups milk

3 tablespoons butter

½ cup Baileys or other Irish cream liqueur

1 cup strong coffee

1 pint heavy cream

¼ cup sugar

1 teaspoon vanilla extract

1 cup chopped Heath Bars or other toffee

Baked Pears with Mascarpone and Amaretti

We love the concept of poached pears, but they are quite time-consuming. Bake those pears instead. This recipe is absolutely delicious, and the mascarpone and crumbled amaretti cookies really set it apart from other versions.

6 to 8 pears

12 to 16 cloves

1½ cups dark brown sugar

1 cup water

½ cup brandy

1 package (12 ounces) amaretti cookies, crushed

1 container (10 ounces) mascarpone cheese, whipped

1. Preheat the oven to 350°F.

2. Halve the pears and core them. Do not peel. Place them cut side down in a large baking pan. Stick a clove into each of the pear halves.

3. Combine the brown sugar and water in a saucepan and bring the mixture to a boil to make a syrup. Pour the sugar syrup over the pears and bake for about an hour, or until the pears are tender. Remove the baked pears from the oven and pour the brandy over them. This can be done several hours before serving time. Just cover and store the pears in the refrigerator, then let them return to room temperature before serving. They're also great served warm from the oven.

4. At dessert time, place the pears in a bowl. Place the crushed amaretti cookies in a bowl and set them beside the pears, along with a bowl of the whipped mascarpone. You can show your guests how to eat this by placing a pear in a shallow bowl, spooning a little of the syrup over it, and topping it with a dollop of whipped cheese and a sprinkling of the amaretti crumbs. If you do show-and-tell on two or three desserts, everyone will get the picture.

Pumpkin Flan with Sweet Tortilla Chips

This is a nice autumnal twist on a traditional flan: not only is the flavor delicious, but the pumpkin puree creates an appealing texture. Add the crispy cinnamon sugar–coated tortilla chips and you've got a hit on your hands. The chips are an easy version of the classic deep-fried Mexican cookie, the buñuelo, a good textural accompaniment to the creamy flan. Put them out in a basket next to the flan so people can get a spoonful of one with a handful of the other.

To make the chips

1. In a long, shallow baking pan, combine 2 cups of the sugar, the salt, and cinnamon. Add more sugar as you need it, along with a little more salt and cinnamon.

2. In a heavy cast-iron skillet or a heavy saucepan with a wide mouth, heat 2 inches of oil over medium heat. Test a wedge of tortilla to make sure the oil is hot enough—if a single wedge browns in 1 minute, the oil is ready. Put in enough wedges to cover the surface of the oil. Fry the chips, turning them over with long-handled tongs after about 2 minutes.

3. When the chips have browned on both sides, after 2 to 3 minutes more, remove them from the heat and transfer them to the sugar mixture. With your hand or a spoon, coat each chip thoroughly on both sides.

4. When the chips are sugar-coated, place them in a brown paper bag or a serving container (such as a bowl or napkin-linked basket). Continue frying the chips until you have enough for your crowd. Putting them directly in the sugar instead of draining them first seals the sugar mixture right on them. The oil makes the sugar cling—and that's a good thing.

To make the flan

1. Preheat the oven to 350°F.

2. In a heavy saucepan, melt 1 cup of the sugar over low heat, stirring occasionally. When the sugar is a dark caramel color, after 15 to 20 minutes, pour it into the bottom of a large, round casserole dish. The sugar will harden.

3. In another heavy saucepan, bring the milk to a boil. Quickly remove it from the heat, add the vanilla bean and orange zest, cover, and let the milk stand for at least 20 minutes. *(continued)*

FOR THE CHIPS
1 to 2 dozen large flour tortillas, each cut into 8 wedges

2 to 4 cups sugar

¼ cup cinnamon, plus additional if needed

1 tablespoon kosher salt, plus additional if needed

Canola oil, for frying

FOR THE FLAN
1²⁄₃ cups sugar

1 quart (4 cups) milk

1 vanilla bean, split

Zest of 1 orange

4 eggs

4 egg yolks

1 can (15 ounces) pumpkin puree

2 tablespoons chopped candied ginger

4. In a mixing bowl, beat together the eggs, egg yolk, and remaining ²/₃ cup sugar. Add the pumpkin and candied ginger. When the milk has steeped, pour a small amount of it through a strainer into the egg mixture. Continue to strain and add the steeped milk to the egg mixture slowly so as not to cook the eggs prematurely. When all the ingredients are combined, pour the custard into the casserole, on top of the hardened sugar.

5. Place the casserole in a large baking pan, put them in the oven, and then pour enough water into the baking pan to come halfway up the sides of the casserole. Bake the flan in this water bath until the custard is set in the middle and doesn't jiggle when gently shaken, about 90 minutes. When the flan is done, remove it from the water bath, cool, and chill it for 2 hours or overnight. At dessert time, invert the flan onto a big platter and serve with the sugar-coated tortilla chips on the side.

Aunt Mayme's Date Pudding

Lulu's Aunt Mayme was known for two culinary treats: her apples baked with Red Hots (she put the candies where the core was) and this date pudding. It really isn't a pudding as we know pudding, more like a cake enveloping dates and walnuts. Serve it with a little dollop of whipped cream or some bourbon sauce. It is perfect for winter dinner parties or a holiday feast because it takes very little time to put together.

---

4 eggs, beaten

1½ cups sugar

²/₃ cup milk

1 cup all-purpose flour

3 teaspoons baking powder

1½ cups walnut pieces or halves, chopped

2 cups dried dates, chopped

Butter or nonstick baking spray, for the pan

1. Preheat the oven to 350°F.

2. In a large mixing bowl, combine all the ingredients thoroughly. The flour seems to want to get caught in the dates, so if you don't mix thoroughly, there will be smudges of uncooked flour in the finished product!

3. Grease or spray a 9 x 13-inch baking dish and pour the date mixture into it. Bake until a toothpick comes out clean when inserted in the center, 40 to 50 minutes.

Viola's Fruitcake

Lulu received this recipe from a neighbor in her teenage bride days. She forgot about it for years but recently made a couple of these cakes for a holiday dessert party as a joke. She found to her amazement that the fruitcakes were the hit of the table—only a slice or two were left. Lulu brought those home for us to taste, and we decided everyone should have a good fruitcake recipe in their repertoire. Of course, Lulu modernized it a bit with dried papaya and pineapple, unavailable years ago.

1. Preheat the oven to 300°F.

2. Grease or spray two loaf pans with nonstick baking spray. Line them with parchment paper so that the sides of the paper come up over the top of the pans.

3. Combine the nuts and fruits in a large mixing bowl. Add the dry ingredients (flour, sugar, baking powder, and salt) and toss until the fruit and nuts are coated. Stir in the eggs and vanilla.

4. Divide the mixture between the two pans. This is better than one big, thick fruitcake, as a big fruitcake is much harder to slice.

5. Bake for 1 hour, then fold the parchment paper over the top of the cake so the nuts don't burn. Continue cooking for about 1½ hours, until a toothpick comes out clean when inserted in the center of the cake.

6. When you remove the cakes from the oven, splash them with brandy. Let them cool in the pans and absorb the brandy. After they have cooled, pull out the cakes by the parchment paper, then peel the paper off. Cover them with plastic wrap and store until needed. Neighbor Viola, now sadly passed on, claimed you could keep this cake for 2 or 3 months in the refrigerator! We've found it gets devoured long before that. You can easily make it a week or so before you are serving it.

Butter or nonstick baking spray, for the pans

1½ cups whole Brazil nuts

1½ cups walnut halves

8 ounces whole pitted dates

1 cup dried fruit: we used a combination of papaya and pineapple and avoided the dried and candied orange peel that is the downfall of some fruitcakes

½ cup each of red maraschino cherries and green maraschino cherries, drained

½ cup raisins

¾ cup all-purpose flour, sifted

¾ cup sugar

½ teaspoon each of baking powder and kosher salt

3 eggs, beaten until fluffy

1 teaspoon vanilla extract

Brandy

Parchment paper, for lining the pans

Bread Pudding with Pears and Pine Nuts

Our friend Susan Sanchez, a gifted pastry chef, shared the basic recipe for this custardy bread pudding. We tarted it up with the pears and the pine nuts, and because we love pears and caramel together, we added some caramel sauce to drizzle over the pudding. Just put it out on the serving table in its baking dish with some plates and a bowl of the sauce, and you have a great serve-it-yourself sweet.

---

1 loaf thin-sliced raisin-cinnamon bread, crusts on

1 quart half-and-half

2 cups heavy cream

1 cup sugar

7 eggs, beaten

6 egg yolks, beaten

1 teaspoon vanilla extract

2 baking pears (Bosc or Anjou work well), chopped

½ cup lightly toasted pine nuts (see page 38)

1 recipe Caramel Sauce (recipe follows)

1. Cut the slices of bread in half. Arrange them in a lasagna pan or large (12- or 14-inch) round casserole dish with the points up, overlapping.

2. In a heavy saucepan, over low heat bring the half-and-half, cream, and sugar to a boil. Remove from the heat. Beat the eggs and egg yolks together in a large mixing bowl. Add a small amount of the hot cream to the egg mixture, then slowly combine the rest of the eggs and cream so the eggs don't cook prematurely. Stir in the vanilla.

3. Preheat the oven to 325°F. Arrange the chopped pears and toasted pine nuts on top of the bread. Pour the custard through a strainer over the bread.

4. Gently push the bread slices into the custard so the liquid is absorbed. Give the pudding about 10 minutes to soak up the moisture, and then bake for about an hour, until the pudding is set. If you have another, larger, baking dish, you can bake the pudding in a hot water bath. We didn't have a big enough pan the last time we made it, but it turned out fine, better than fine. Delicious, in fact. Serve warm or at room temperature.

Caramel Sauce

1 cup dark brown sugar

¼ cup sugar

Dash of kosher salt

½ cup corn syrup

1 cup heavy cream

Combine all the ingredients in a heavy saucepan. Cook over medium heat until the sugar melts, then reduce the heat to low and simmer until the sauce turns a lovely caramel color, about 20 minutes.

Big Platter Ingredients

The world is definitely getting smaller when it comes to the availability of exotic ingredients. Items that used to be available only in ethnic markets (or not at all) are now just a click away on the Internet and are increasingly found in chain supermarkets. If your market doesn't stock some of the following ingredients, talk to the manager and suggest that the store should carry them; grocers who want your repeat business will be happy to special-order products for you. The following list describes some of the items we simply wouldn't be without.

Black Sesame Seeds: These are available in Asian grocery stores, some well-stocked supermarkets, and online. Black sesame seeds are less common than the white ones and have a slightly more concentrated flavor. They pack a punch both visually and flavor-wise when used as a garnish. In China, meat and fish are rolled in the black seeds before cooking to create a crunchy coating. In Japan, black sesame seeds are used in rice and noodle dishes and as a tabletop condiment. Because of their high oil content, sesame seeds can quickly turn rancid. To avoid this, store them in a cool, dark place for up to three months, refrigerate for up to six months, or freeze for up to one year.

Kosher Salt: A discussion of salt could fill an entire book (in fact, it already has), but suffice it to say that we favor kosher salt because the special shape of the flakes gives maximum salt flavor for the minimum amount used. But don't believe us, try your own taste test: Pour out a little iodized salt and a little kosher salt. Taste a small amount of each. We think you'll agree that the kosher salt has a light, fresh salt flavor, far preferable to the processed taste of the other.

Lemon Grass: Lemon grass plays a pivotal role in flavoring Thai food. It looks a little like a sturdy green onion, with long, thin leaves and a slightly bulbous base. The white bulbous portion is responsible for the sour lemon flavor and fragrance. Readily available fresh at Asian markets and some well-stocked supermarkets, you can also find it in its dried form in Thai markets.

Rice Wine Vinegar: Rice wine vinegar has a taste similar to white wine vinegar, but it is higher in vinegar content. Oddly enough, it tastes less acidic and milder in flavor than Western vinegars, probably due to the hint of sweetness that comes from the glutinous rice from which it is made. Seasoned rice wine vinegar usually contains both salt and sugar, and may include other flavors, such as ginger.

Sesame Oil and Toasted Sesame Oil: Both versions of this very tasty oil are expressed from, you guessed it, sesame seeds. The flavor that is so appealing on that hamburger bun dotted with sesame seeds is the same one you'll get when using sesame oil. Intensely flavored, a little goes a long way. To continue the analogy, toasted sesame oil has the flavor of a toasted hamburger bun—even more intensified in flavor and darker in color than regular sesame oil. You can find both in Asian markets and well-stocked supermarkets.

Sriracha Chili-Garlic Sauce: First of all, it's pronounced *sree-rah-chah*. But everyone seems to call it "red rooster sauce" because it's red and the most common brand has a rooster on the label. A combination of red chiles, garlic, salt, sugar, and vinegar, it's the hot sauce that's taking the country by storm, challenging the dominance of the venerable Tabasco brand. First marketed in Southern California some 20 years ago by a Vietnamese refugee named David Tran, this sauce has never been advertised. But word-of-mouth has made it one of the most popular hot sauces nationwide, selling over $7 million worth last year. Formerly found only in Asian restaurants and grocery stores, sriracha sauce is now available nationwide, particularly in well-stocked supermarkets.

Thai Sweet Chili Sauce (*Mae Ploy*): Sweet, tart, hot—this odd combination of flavors (at least from a Western point of view) makes Thai sweet chili sauce indispensable to Thai cuisine and provides the complexity so identified with it. Talk about a flavor booster! This chili sauce has the potential to become your "secret ingredient" in everything from barbecue sauces to marinades to salad dressings. It is widely available in Asian markets and most well-stocked supermarkets.

Big Platter Pots, Pans, and Platters

Before it lands on a big platter, the food presented in this book must be prepared, and we're here to tell you that a few slightly oversized pots and pans make that preparation a whole lot easier. The list is mercifully short, but if your inclination or budget requires an even shorter list, we believe that the 15-inch cast-iron frying pan is the most versatile, and least expensive, of our recommendations. In it, you can cook a big batch of flapjacks, brown stew meat, simmer a sauce, or sauté several heads of broccoli at the same time. It can do all of this, and it's so long-lasting your grandkids will probably be using it when they're grandparents!

16-Quart Aluminum Stockpot with Lid: Every kitchen should have one big stockpot, large enough to cook up a couple pounds of pasta at one time, chili for the entire Girl Scout troop, or turkey soup made from the entire Thanksgiving turkey carcass. Widely available in restaurant supply stores, kitchen shops, and online, we've found many offered for less than $30, including the lid! You'll be glad you have this pot in your kitchen arsenal, even if you use it only a couple of times a year.

Le Creuset 13-Quart Covered Round French Oven: We don't often suggest brand-name items, but the Le Creuset line of pots and pans is so unique, no other brand can compare. These very heavy-duty pots from France are constructed from enameled cast iron and are built to last a lifetime or two. The bottoms of the pans are extra-thick, making them perfect for browning meats. And the handles on the lids are heat-resistant, which means you can place the covered pot in the oven without fear of damage. Cooking oxtails, short ribs, lamb shanks, or osso buco is a pure pleasure in this beautiful pan. The only drawback is they're about as expensive as they are heavy . . . but worth the cost.

18-Inch Paella Pan: This pan was a surprise to us. We were wandering around a Spanish food store and happened on stacks of paella pans, in every different size imaginable. They were beautifully constructed of Teflon-coated aluminum, thick enough to say "serious cooking." We hadn't decided to include paella in the cookbook yet, but we decided to right then and there. The other surprise was that the 18-inch size fits perfectly on a standard 22-inch diameter kettle grill, making it the perfect pan for cooking paella over a live fire. This is a very versatile pan: Just think of it as an oversized, well-constructed sauté pan.

15-Inch Cast-Iron Frying Pan: First off, we should warn you that this pan weighs (in pounds) almost as much as its diameter in inches—definitely a two-handed lift from the cupboard to the stove. But, as we noted in the introduction, this is our favorite all-purpose pan and we simply wouldn't be without it. Available at hardware stores, kitchen shops, and online (although the postage will probably cost more than pan itself), take good care of this baby and it will take good care of you.

15-Inch Cazuela: This traditional terra-cotta casserole dish from Spain is as beautiful as it is useful. It is glazed on the inside and unglazed on the bottom. Because it's fired at relatively low temperatures (around 200°F), this dish needs some special handling when you first bring it home. It should be soaked in water for six hours prior to first use. If you live in a very dry climate, you may want to resoak it occasionally. Once its moisture content is restored, it can be used over a direct flame (gas or electric range) on low to medium heat (high heat is not recommended), in the oven, or in the microwave. It may be washed in the dishwasher if it is placed so the rim does not bang against another dish. It also helps to put your cazuela in a cold oven the first few times you use it to let it warm up gradually as the oven preheats. Available in a wide range of sizes, we found the 15-inch model perfect for Big Platter dishes.

Collecting Platters: Now comes the fun part: collecting platters on which to serve your Big Platter food. To begin, we recommend two sets: three splatter-ware tin platters and three white platters with a lip. For inspiration, there's our friend Lennie, a former gallery owner whose platters are a "who's who" of contemporary American ceramics. Then there's Sally, who has some of the most beautiful hand-painted Italian platters you ever saw. Lulu collects hers from estates sales and antique malls, while Cort is a purist: he loves all white platters. All of these collections set tables that reflect the personalities of their owners. When you're traveling, attending antique, art, or craft shows, or shopping at discount stores such as Ross, T.J. Maxx, or Marshalls, think platters. The next thing you know, a collection will be born.

Acknowledgments

As much as we'd like to claim that this book is the result of logical choices and deliberate action, as is the case with many projects like this, it actually came into being after a string of happy accidents. With that in mind, we'd like to thank Rozanne Gold for getting our idea in front of our very capable and gracious editor (and publisher), Leslie Stoker, and also our agent, Lisa Queen, for shepherding the book into reality.

Thanks also to Gena Allen, Jorge Velazquez, and the rest of the crew at the incomparable Sunshine Foods in St. Helena for carrying the kinds of food we like to cook. And thanks, Laura Rombauer, proprietor of Napa Valley Vintage Home, for coming through with props when we really needed them, and John Sorenson for the "loan" of his great wines. For her incomparable enthusiasm and humor, many thanks to our own private cheerleader, Little Debbie, and her teammate, Super Dave, for his patience and hospitality.

We'd still be eating leftovers without our roving team of Good Eaters. Thanks to the elite of Napa County's Sheriff's Department: Captain and Mrs. (Denise) Loughran, Undersheriff and Mrs. (Cindy) York, and Captain and Mrs. (Kelli) Lyerla; to Tom and Nushi, Tim and Cindy, Genie and Will, Andrew and Debra, Sean and Laura, Tom and Linda, and Rick and Chris. To the photographic crew—Steven Rothfeld, David Shalleck, and Chuck Luter—thanks for making everything look so good and groovin' to the music. And finally, hats off to project editor Sarah Scheffel for making it all make sense in the end!

Metric Conversion Chart

VOLUME EQUIVALENTS

These are not exact equivalents for American cups and spoons, but have been rounded up or down slightly to make measuring easier.

American	Metric	Imperial
¼ t	1.2 ml	
½ t	2.5 ml	
1 t	5.0 ml	
½ T (1.5 t)	7.5 ml	
1 T (3 t)	15 ml	
¼ cup (4 T)	60 ml	2 fl oz
⅓ cup (5 T)	75 ml	2½ fl oz
½ cup (8 T)	125 ml	4 fl oz
⅔ cup (10 T)	150 ml	5 fl oz
¾ cup (12 T)	175 ml	6 fl oz
1 cup (16 T)	250 ml	8 fl oz
1¼ cups	300 ml	10 fl oz (½ pt)
1½ cups	350 ml	12 fl oz
2 cups (1 pint)	500 ml	16 fl oz
2½ cups	625 ml	20 fl oz (1 pint)
1 quart	1 liter	32 fl oz

OVEN TEMPERATURE EQUIVALENTS

Oven Mark	F	C	Gas
Very cool	250–275	130–140	½–1
Cool	300	150	2
Warm	325	170	3
Moderate	350	180	4
Moderately hot	375	190	5
	400	200	6
Hot	425	220	7
	450	230	8
Very hot	475	250	9

WEIGHT EQUIVALENTS

The metric weights given in this chart are not exact equivalents, but have been rounded up or down slightly to make measuring easier.

Avoirdupois	Metric
¼ oz	7 g
½ oz	15 g
1 oz	30 g
2 oz	60 g
3 oz	90 g
4 oz	115 g
5 oz	150 g
6 oz	175 g
7 oz	200 g
8 oz (½ lb)	225 g
9 oz	250 g
10 oz	300 g
11 oz	325 g
12 oz	350 g
13 oz	375 g
14 oz	400 g
15 oz	425 g
16 oz (1 lb)	450 g
1½ lb	750 g
2 lb	900 g
2¼ lb	1 kg
3 lb	1.4 kg
4 lb	1.8 kg

Index

Page numbers in *italics* refer to photographs.